Critical Guides to French Texts

33 Anouilh: L'Alouette *and* Pauvre Bitos

Critical Guides to French Texts

EDITED BY ROGER LITTLE, WOLFGANG VAN EMDEN, DAVID WILLIAMS

ANOUILH

L'Alouette *and* Pauvre Bitos

S. Beynon John

Reader in French,
University of Sussex

Grant & Cutler Ltd
1984

© Grant & Cutler Ltd
  1984
ISBN 0 7293 0169 9

I.S.B.N. 84-499-6885-2

DEPÓSITO LEGAL: V. 88 - 1984

Printed in Spain by
Artes Gráficas Soler, S.A., Valencia
for
GRANT & CUTLER LTD
11 BUCKINGHAM STREET, LONDON W.C.2

Contents

Contents

Prefatory Note

The editions of the two plays used in this study are the current paperback reprints of the following:

L'Alouette, ed. Merlin Thomas & Simon Lee (London, Methuen, 1956).

Pauvre Bitos ou le dîner de têtes, ed. W.D. Howarth (London, Harrap, 1958).

Quotations from other plays by Anouilh are taken from the appropriate volumes of his collected plays, full details of which are listed in the select bibliography. The titles of the volumes I quote from are abbreviated as follows in the body of my text:

Pièces noires: *PN*

Nouvelles pièces noires: *NPN*

Pièces brillantes: *PB*

Pièces costumées: *PC*

When plays are mentioned initially the date of the first performance is given in brackets after the title. The figures in parenthesis in italic type refer to numbered items in the select bibliography; the italic figure is usually followed by a page reference. The bibliography represents a limited and personal choice, though I have tried to include a variety of approaches and some suggestions for further reading. I have placed an asterisk beside the critical studies I have found most useful. My debts to other critics are reflected in the bibliography, but I occasionally give a specific reference in a footnote when I have borrowed facts or insights that seemed to me especially useful or suggestive.

I am most grateful to the Advisory Editor, Professor Roger Little, for his forbearance and to Yvonne Hope and Helen Howard for their skilful typing of the manuscript.

1. History as Metaphor

(i)

L'Alouette (1953) and *Pauvre Bitos ou le dîner de têtes* (1956): here are two plays by Anouilh, performed soon after each other, that appear to form a natural pair. Both are ostensibly rooted in French history (the fifteenth century and the period of the French Revolution); neither is, in fact, a historical play in the proper sense, though both exhibit in style and temper a kind of family likeness with a group of post-war plays that exploit historical subject-matter in a very individual way: *Becket ou l'honneur de Dieu* (1959), *La Foire d'empoigne* (1962), *Le Boulanger, la boulangère et le petit mitron* (1968), *La Belle Vie* (1979). I do not find in either play any real curiosity about the past or any serious attempt to enter imaginatively into historical periods remote from us and to make those worlds, with their distinctive idioms, hierarchies and beliefs, come alive for us. Indeed, to judge from these plays, Anouilh seems to be saying not that the past is another country where they do things differently, but that it is literally irretrievable for us except in terms of popular iconography and the crudely simplified notions of morality and society we derive from national folklore. It would only be a slight exaggeration to assert that Anouilh's principal historical figures tend to be represented in the primary colours and naïve stereotypes of the *images d'Epinal*, those cheap prints that spoke so vigorously to the popular mind of the early nineteenth century. As a matter of fact, the stage directions for Anouilh's historical comedy about Napoleon, *La Foire d'empoigne*, specifically call for this kind of stylization: 'Tous les personnages ont les traits un peu grossis, des ventres exagérés comme sur les caricatures anglaises de l'époque.' (*PC*, p.303).

Certainly such figures are very strongly conventionalized by Anouilh, and the significance of such an approach seems to rest on a view of human nature as essentially unchanging and on a preference for using history as metaphor, as a way of illuminating our present idealisms, allegiances and treacheries. More specifically, I would want to argue that Anouilh is moved to revive these exemplary figures of the French past not merely out of a general or abstract interest in good and evil, means and ends, but out of his own experience of the savage conflicts which divided Frenchmen during the German Occupation of France, 1940-1944 and its aftermath. In a word, *L'Alouette* and *Pauvre Bitos* are haunted by echoes of occupation, collaboration and resistance in France and articulate for us the voices of conscience and expediency, principle and fanaticism. In this sense, the fates of Joan of Arc and Robespierre are, to a significant degree, though not exclusively, metaphors for the political divisions of our own times.

In connecting the 'history' of these plays with the conflicts of Vichy France (1940-1944) it will be convenient to look first at the political mythologies which crystallize around Joan of Arc. The successive metamorphoses which the figure of Joan has undergone since her trial and burning in the fifteenth century themselves constitute a fascinating story. In popular iconography she has been represented in many forms, from warlike Amazon armed with a bow, or dashing equestrian warrior, to simple peasant girl, saintly martyr, and personification of the Republic.[1] But in seeking to explain Anouilh's choice of Joan as the subject for a play, one needs to look briefly at the role played by Joan of Arc in French political life since the late nineteenth century, and to show how this connects with the politics of Vichy France. In modern times the figure of Joan has never been free of political controversy in her own country. In the wake of France's defeat in the Franco-Prussian War of 1870 and the terrible repression of the Paris Commune in 1871, a deeply conservative régime was set up under a reactionary soldier-president, Marshal MacMahon. Frenchmen were urged by the Catholic Church to perform a great act of repentance so as to

[1] These cultural metamorphoses are suggestively explored in Marina Warner's *Joan of Arc* (9).

atone for the sins which, it was alleged, had brought about their national disasters. The call was ardently taken up by conservative and clerical groups and found expression in a growing cult of the Sacred Heart, linked to the sorrows of France, a campaign to erect the Sacré-Cœur church on the heights of Montmartre, and mass pilgrimages to Lourdes and other shrines which were organized by the Order of the Assumptionists. These developments were accompanied by an intensification of the cult of Joan of Arc, and one can judge something of the popular fervour from the success that greeted Jules Barbier's *Jeanne d'Arc*, set to music by Gounod and first performed in Paris in 1873. The strenuous efforts made by clericalists and royalists to capture Joan for the cause of conservative nationalism, to associate her indelibly with throne and altar, and to replace the patriotic rituals associated with the anniversary of the Fall of the Bastille on 14 July 1789 with a religious festival in honour of Joan, the 'envoy of God', were countered by the activities of ardent republicans and free-thinkers who struggled to conscript Joan for the cause of a secular republic and to establish a national day in honour of the 'saviour of the nation'.[2]

There are striking affinities between the political climate of the eighteen seventies and that of Vichy France. The French military collapse of June 1940 brought in its train the downfall of the Third Republic and the partial, subsequently total, occupation of France by the Germans. As after 1870, a conservative and authoritarian régime, hostile to republicanism and to parliamentary democracy, was set up — this time under the aged Marshal Pétain. Essentially, the Pétain government looked for inspiration to the reactionary doctrines of nationalism associated with extreme right-wing political groups of the late nineteenth century, and specifically, to Charles Maurras, the deaf and fanatical ideologist of the monarchist and antisemitic Action Française, who, in old age, enjoyed a spell of power as the semi-official philosopher of the Vichy régime.

---

[2] Rosemonde Sanson, 'La fête de Jeanne d'Arc en 1894, controverse et célé-bration', *Revue d'histoire moderne et contemporaine*, XX (July-September 1973), 444-63.

The struggle between French political parties to acquire
prescriptive rights over Joan of Arc as a symbol of patriotism
and national unity, which was so bitter in the last quarter of the
nineteenth century, flares up again in the conflict between
Pétain and de Gaulle during the Second World War. This battle
of symbols is epitomized in the clash between the German
propaganda poster featuring the prayerful figure of the saint at
the stake, superimposed on images of Rouen burning under
Allied bombs, and the Gaullist poster in which the image of
Joan's martyrdom is associated with the cross of her home
province of Lorraine, the emblem of the Free French movement.
As for the plays themselves, the Parisian public was allowed to
see, in the earliest days of the German occupation, a performance of Bernard Shaw's *Saint Joan* (Théâtre de l'Avenue,
December 1940), and a production of Charles Péguy's *Jeanne
d'Arc* at the Théâtre Hébertot (1941). Claudel's own *Jeanne
d'Arc au bûcher*, a 'dramatic oratorio' was staged at Lyons, in
the unoccupied zone, in a performance he disowned (July 1941)
before being given a successful Parisian production at the
Théâtre National Populaire (June 1942) and a memorable radio
broadcast in May 1943, conducted by Honegger who had
composed the music. Among the wartime plays about Joan, one
of the most subversive, in the sense of being aimed as much at
the German invaders as at the traditional English enemy, was the
unknown Claude Vermorel's *Jeanne avec nous*. This was staged
in January 1942 under the auspices of the Vichy-subsidized
'Société du théâtre d'essai' at the Comédie des Champs-Elysées.
It seems to me to offer some affinities with *L'Alouette*, and I
shall return to these.

It is not difficult to guess what prompted the German censors
to license Shaw's *Saint Joan* for performance: it was the work of
a witty Irishman who had long been the gadfly of British society,
and its sympathetic understanding of Joan's plight, combined
with a robust satire of English cant, self-interest and perfidy,
made it a perfect instrument for reviving anti-English sentiment
in German-occupied Paris. Of course, there was a certain
naïveté on the part of the German Propaganda-Staffel in failing
to realize that the legend of Joan, in whatever guise, would be

certain to contribute significantly to the French sense of national identity and solidarity in the face of their immediate oppressors. What is more, plays about the 'Maid of Orleans' were entirely consistent with the Vichy government's policy of stimulating and sustaining patriotic feeling by appeals to the glorious past that associated French greatness with the practice and institutions of the Catholic religion and their related insistence on authority and social hierarchy. In fact, within France, Joan became very much the property of the Right, as was only to be expected of a régime which hoped to put into effect the principles of integral nationalism preached by the pre-war Action Française. In this context it is worth recalling the enthusiastic celebrations of Joan of Arc which were organized throughout France, in May 1942, and which took the form of processions, lectures and poetry-readings, as well as musical and dramatic performances.[3]

It seems to me that the special resonance and poignancy with which the circumstances of the German Occupation invested stage performances about Joan of Arc must account in large part for Anouilh's decision to create *L'Alouette* a few years after the liberation of France. He is likely to have responded to the evident power of the legend to transcend conventional piety and to speak directly and meaningfully to a contemporary audience. Perhaps, too, the plays produced in those sombre days served to remind Anouilh of the great tradition of imaginative writing devoted to Joan, from Voltaire, Schiller, Michelet and Péguy to twentieth century dramatists who had responded to the fascination of her legend. Apart from Shaw's own polemical version (1924), which almost certainly figured among the 'dog-eared' copies of Shaw's plays which Anouilh carried around in his pockets as a young man in the nineteen twenties (7, p.168), the twentieth-century repertory ranges from Brecht's *St Joan of the Stockyards* (1929-30) and Maxwell Anderson's *Joan of Lorraine* (1946), to two plays by French contemporaries of Anouilh which immediately preceded his own: Jacques Audiberti's *Pucelle* (1950) and Thierry Maulnier's *Jeanne et les*

[3] Patrick Marsh, 'Jeanne d'Arc during the German Occupation', *Theatre Research International*, ns II, 2 (February 1977), 140-42.

juges (1950). As if these versions did not provide a sufficient challenge to a dramatist fast emerging as a master of his craft, and acutely aware of the theatrical tradition to which he belonged, the legend was to be revived in the most graphic form when, in 1952, Anouilh was involved in dubbing the Rossellini/ Ingrid Bergman screen version of Claudel's *Jeanne au bûcher*. The experience of this new film seems to have clinched matters for Anouilh, making him readier to accept the advice offered by a Jesuit priest (R.P. Doncœur) to tackle the subject for himself. As Doncœur put it: 'Justement, Jeanne est l'Antigone chrétienne' (7, p.221). It is a judgement which neatly connects the moral conflicts of *L'Alouette* with those of Anouilh's great wartime success *Antigone* (1944), and it suggests the degree to which the themes of conscience, integrity and judicial murder which occur in *L'Alouette* are rooted in the experience of the Occupation.

So I would say that the accident of being involved in the Ingrid Bergman film, the challenge offered by other treatments of the legend, the spell of those powerful associations linking Joan of Arc with the national crisis of 1940-44, all impelled Anouilh toward writing his own 'Saint Joan'. But it is the clash between the rival political factions within wartime France, and their associated ethical conflicts and ambiguities, which emerges as crucial in helping to define the moral argument, dominant tone and emphases which characterize both *L'Alouette* and *Pauvre Bitos*. In this respect, the career and fate of the French writer, Fascist sympathizer and collaborator, Robert Brasillach, seem to me to connect private and public life for Anouilh in a peculiarly vivid way and to determine how he came to view the Occupation's conflicts of allegiance. In fact, I would suggest that the ghost of Brasillach lies behind the more intense moments of both plays, especially when they dwell on the relations between personal integrity and the claims of ideology, private conscience and the demands of the state.

This is no place to rehearse in detail the exact nature of the ideological differences between clandestine resistance groups, the obscurantist nationalists and conservatives of the Pétain régime, caught up in an uneasy and compromising relationship with the German occupying authorities, and the pro-Fascist collaborationists of Paris, deeply antisemitic and pledged to making France part of the Nazi 'New Order' in Europe. It is enough to recall that the Paris collaborationists were doctrinaire fanatics, disproportionately influential in the world of journalism, and that Brasillach belonged to them. Brasillach, who was a talented novelist, critic and historian of the cinema, was a great admirer of Nazi Germany, bitterly critical of the French republican and parliamentary system, and a virulent antisemite.

Soon after the Vichy government had intervened to secure his early release from a prisoner of war camp in 1940, Brasillach resumed his post as editor in chief of the extreme Right-wing paper *Je suis partout* (April 1941) and became a fervent spokesman for Franco-German collaboration. The strength of his commitment to the New Order was such that within a year he was arguing strenuously for the creation of a truly fascist France, modelled on the Third Reich and linked with Germany in a fascist Europe. Convinced that the future of fascism lay with the Nazi conquerors, Brasillach was prepared to give total support to the German occupying power. By the summer of 1943 Brasillach had become sceptical of a German victory but continued to express his close identification with the German cause. Imprisoned and put on trial for treason at the Liberation, he was condemned and executed at the fortress of Montrouge on 6 February 1945.[4]

The execution of Brasillach became a *cause célèbre* in postwar France. Predictably his death was condemned as an act of political revenge by a motley crowd of right-wing sympathizers, many with questionable wartime records. But others, with more respectable credentials, were also ready to argue that Brasillach's activities were mistaken rather than treasonable, that a fair trial was impossible in the wake of the Occupation, and that consequently his execution was an act of judicial murder. Certainly Brasillach was seen on the Right as the victim

[4] A detached and useful account of Brasillach's career is given in William R. Tucker, *The Fascist Ego: a political biography of Robert Brasillach* (Berkeley, University of California Press, 1975).

of a conspiracy by the Communist Party which had emerged
victorious from the French resistance movement and was
determined to take revenge on wartime collaborators. The
parallel with *Pauvre Bitos* is at its most obvious here. Anouilh,
who seems not to have known Brasillach well, was active in
canvassing signatures for an (abortive) petition for clemency.
The whole question of Brasillach's guilt and execution is
extremely complicated, but it is certain that it had a profound
effect on Anouilh whose own political sympathies were investi-
gated in the aftermath of the Liberation. As Anouilh was to
write later, he felt that Brasillach's death coincided with the end
of his own youth, that the authorities who condemned him were
discredited by their decision, and that Brasillach transcended
himself in death and rose above hatred: 'Le petit garçon qui
regardait la mort en face reste debout et intact — éternellement',
and 'Cet enfant nu d'un matin de février (car je crois qu'il est
resté un enfant, c'est pour cela qu'il n'a pas haï, qu'il leur a
tendu la main et qu'il a crié: Vive la France!)...' (7, p.176 &
p.178).

I have to say that though these images of childlike innocence
are entirely consistent with the cult of childhood and adolescence that everywhere pervades Brasillach's own fiction and
autobiographical writings, Anouilh's reference to them seems to
me cheaply sentimentalized, religiose, and quite unrelated to
Brasillach's public career, the egoism and opportunism he
frequently displayed in the sphere of journalism, and the
ferocity of his denunciations of resisters, freemasons,
communists and Jews at a time when verbal incitements could
have lethal consequences. In a word, I think Anouilh quite
mistaken in his judgement of Brasillach as some sort of heedless
child who had wandered by accident into the murderous world
of adults. However, it is clear that his image of Brasillach as a
victim of political intrigue, an idealist perhaps led astray by a
vision of Franco-German friendship but dying faithful to the
'voices' of his dream, is a vital element in colouring the conflicts
of principle and loyalty we encounter in *L'Alouette* and *Pauvre
Bitos*.

I have elaborated this distinctively political context because I see it as the necessary prelude to a proper understanding of the arguments and assumptions which provide the sub-text of *L'Alouette* and *Pauvre Bitos*. For Anouilh the past is not important in itself but only as a way of commenting on the present. This is not at all the same thing as trying to understand the present in the light of the past, but rather a way of drawing on popular images and associations derived from the past in order to reinforce one's present sympathies and convictions. So any expectation that Anouilh will observe scrupulous fidelity to the historical record is not simply misplaced but irrelevant. What matters for the spectator of the plays is the significance to be attached to Anouilh's departures from historical fact.

(ii)

Anouilh himself stresses the spontaneity of his approach to the subject of Joan of Arc. *L'Alouette* was begun at his country house in Montfort-L'Amaury, next to the village church. The bell rang for the Angelus: '... sans plan, sans dates, sans documents, sur mes souvenirs de petit garçon, sans rien qu'une inexplicable joie — je commençai *L'Alouette*' (7, p.221). This highly personal and impressionistic approach is, if anything, reinforced by the sort of historian to whom Anouilh turns for fuller information. His preference runs to historical narratives that are archaic, picturesque and highly literary: Augustin Thierry for *Becket*, Michelet for *L'Alouette*. As is the case with Bernard Shaw's *Saint Joan*, Anouilh wastes no time on the intricacies of the conflict between the Burgundian and Armagnac factions in the political life of the fifteenth century. All that we need to know to follow both Shaw's and Anouilh's plays is the bare bones of Joan's life: Joan of Arc, a farmer's daughter from Domrémy, was born about 1412. Believing herself to be sent by God, she was entrusted by the Dauphin Charles with the command of his troops and raised the siege of Orleans in May 1429, driving the English from their strongholds along the Loire. As a consequence, Charles VII was crowned king at Rheims in July 1429. Joan subsequently failed in a series of military actions and was captured at Compiègne in May 1430, brought to trial, condemned and burnt for heresy, witchcraft and sorcery at Rouen in 1431; rehabilitated after an ecclesiastical inquiry in 1456, and eventually designated a saint in 1920.

The striving for economy and simplicity is further reflected in Anouilh's marked concentration of the conflict between the individual and ecclesiastical institutions, between private 'voices' and religious orthodoxy. The need to create a spare and economical dramatic structure leads Anouilh, like Shaw, to exclude the detail of the seventy original counts on which she was tried. He never loses sight of the primacy of dramatic effect and so discards issues that loom large in the historical transcripts and are repeatedly reverted to. So we hear nothing, in Anouilh's version, of the rusted sword found behind the altar at Saint-Catherine-de-Fierbois, nor of the devices and motto on Joan's battle standard which gave rise to criticism, nor of her alleged raising of a child from the dead at Lagny, nor of her relations with the visionary Catherine de la Rochelle, nor of her making war on the Feast of the Nativity of our Lady, nor of her preference for frequent communion. In these respects, Anouilh's single-minded concern for aesthetic criteria in the making of his play obliges him to be, in the broadest sense, anachronistic; that is, to depart from the theological spirit of the fifteenth century, to ignore questions about false prophecy or excessive devotional zeal, and greatly to diminish the medieval fear of demons and dread of witchcraft. Unlike Shaw, Anouilh shows Joan being interrogated about the village girls' games around the 'Arbre aux fées', but the incident (p.45) is so quickly and lightly disposed of by Cauchon ('Il nous faut laisser quelques fées aux petites filles, dans notre propre intérêt') that nothing emerges of that medieval suspicion of the malefic powers of woods: 'du côté de l'obscur, du magique, du diabolique — du côté de la superstition, de la sorcellerie — et de l'hérésie, ce qui est tout un' (2, p.41). For Anouilh's purpose — the dramatic contrast between simple faith and the tyrannical power of institutions — it does not matter whether Joan's religious practice conforms to the norm for good Christians of her period or whether she has been influenced by the sermons of mendicant friars toward a suspect kind of fervour, or whether she belongs to the tradition of mystical prophets, so important, according to Warner, in the fourteenth century (*9*, p.89). He is not concerned with the *context* of her beliefs, only with their force and sincerity, and so does not even exploit dramatically the parallel with St Margaret of whom a statue existed in the church at Domrémy and who had left her matrimonial home dressed in male attire and with her hair cropped short (*2*, p.30). In a word, Anouilh is not interested in showing Joan to be a product of the popular culture of her time, but as special, unique, transcending time and place. Certainly he does not violate the spirit of the medieval polity as grossly as Shaw, when the Irish dramatist, in a witty paradox that runs away with him, makes Joan one of the earliest Protestant martyrs and apostles of modern nationalism. Even so, in presenting Joan as pure individualism at odds with coercive institutions, Anouilh is saying something that is important to the twentieth-century spectator, but quite inappropriate to Joan's own period. The historical Joan did not argue for some alternative system of beliefs but conceived of herself as acting within the limits of medieval Catholicism.

Anouilh follows historical tradition in accepting Joan's virginity (allegations of her being a loose or immoral woman were virtually abandoned during the trial), though without any apparent awareness of, or impulse to dramatize, the fact that prophecies about a virgin-saviour were common currency in the France of the fifteenth century. Like Shaw, he is also faithful to history in accepting that Joan was not a simple shepherdess but the daughter of a substantial farmer, possessed of the domestic skills appropriate to a girl of her station. As she says, with a touch of harmless vanity, both in the original deposition and in Anouilh's play: 'Pour coudre et pour filer, il n'est femme de Rouen qui saurait m'en remontrer' (p.107). Anouilh also grants to Joan's stubborn defence of wearing the uniform of a serving soldier the full importance it is given in the historical trial, recognizing that she identifies male dress with her 'voices', her divinely inspired mission to save France, and her victories in the field. But in giving far less weight to the charges levelled at Joan by her contemporaries of behaving immodestly and demeaning womanhood, of profaning the sacraments by taking them in

male dress, of affecting ostentatious military costume, Anouilh
again affirms his intention not to dramatize Joan's conflict with
the conventions of a feudal and hierarchical society, but to
concentrate on her beliefs, on the battle between private conscience and public dogma.

In *L'Alouette* Anouilh's specific departures from the
historical record not only reinforce the dramatic thrust of the
action but often serve (as we shall see) to assimilate historical
figures to that memorable family of characters he has invented
in his plays, characters who recur persistently and who can be
made to connect the historical and the topical through the
calculated use of what might be called local anachronism; that
is, a highly specific linkage of past with present. Like Shaw,
Anouilh tampers with historical fact so as to present Cauchon in
a very favourable light: he is shown to be gentle, patient and
anxious to safeguard Joan's interests. Certainly there is an
element of historical truth in this, but just as it is vital to the
impact of Shaw's trial scene for Cauchon to appear a well-
intentioned but blinkered servant of the Church confronting
Joan's free spirit, so it is necessary for Anouilh to create an
imaginary Cauchon whose humanity can be contrasted for
dramatic effect with the inhuman fury of the Inquisitor. To
accomplish this, Anouilh has to play down Cauchon's time-
serving, his responsibility for negotiating the transfer of Joan to
English hands, and the report of his reassuring Warwick after
Joan's recantation in the cemetery of the Abbey of Saint-Ouen
on 24 May 1431: 'Monseigneur, ne vous inquiétez pas: nous la
rattraperons bien!' (*1*, p.141). For precisely the same *dramatic*
reason Cauchon is shown as convincing Joan by the power of his
concern and the force of his arguments, whereas the historical
record plainly suggests that she was worn down by physical and
mental exhaustion and by the intimidating prestige and
formality of the tribunal. The significance of this rewriting of
Cauchon's role is articulated through an anachronism which
enables Anouilh to express sympathy for the dilemmas of the
conscientious collaborator caught up in the tides of history. In
presenting Cauchon as bent on safeguarding French interests in
the face of English demands, Anouilh converts this prelate, as he

does his imagined Becket, into a sympathetic figure. In making Cauchon talk anachronistically about being one of the 'collaborateurs sincères du régime anglais' and of living in 'Rouen occupé' (p.70), Anouilh plays up the analogy between the English invader of France in the fifteenth century and the German occupiers of France in the twentieth. Indeed, he reinforces the analogy quite explicitly by allowing Cauchon to conjure up the atmosphere of English occupation in a way that obviously applies to Paris between 1940 and 1944: 'Entouré des soldats de sa Majesté, des exécutions d'otages de sa Majesté. Soumis au couvre-feu et au bon plaisir du ravitaillement de sa Majesté' (p.70). It is difficult not to see in all this that an ideological point of a very twentieth-century kind is being made, and that the dramatist is obliquely defending policies of political collaboration that he found necessary and understandable under the Vichy régime.

Like Shaw again, Anouilh deliberately inflates the role of the Inquisitor for purposes of dramatic contrast, but also so as to make an ideological point. Historically the powers of the French Inquisitor, Jean de Graverent, were delegated throughout the trial to the Vice-Inquisitor, Jean le Maistre, a Dominican monk. To judge from the transcript of the trial, he spoke little, behaved circumspectly, and seems to have had little in common with Anouilh's baleful and unforgiving Inquisitor. Shaw is closer to the record in showing the Inquisitor to be restrained and punctilious, even in the great speech Shaw gives him in Scene 6 when he dilates on the terrible consequences of heresy: 'Anger is a bad counsellor: cast out anger. Pity is sometimes worse: cast out pity. But do not cast out mercy. Remember only that justice comes first' (*5*, p.151). For his part, Anouilh is faithful to history in presenting the Inquisitor as exclusively interested in matters of heresy and witchcraft, but, in intensifying his fanaticism, the playwright consciously departs from history in order to dramatize the debate between simple faith and sophisticated theology and between the vulnerability of the lonely prisoner and the threatening power of official ideology. What is more, the language the Inquisitor employs attains a kind of incandescent abstraction which effectively divorces the

charges he is making from specific religious heresies of the
period so as to make them apply to any kind of dissent,
including the secular and political: '... Si puissants que nous
devenions un jour, sous une forme ou sous une autre, si lourde
que se fasse l'Idée sur le monde, si dures, si précises, si subtiles
que soient son organisation et sa police; il y aura toujours un
homme à chasser quelque part qui lui aura échappé, qu'on
prendra enfin, qu'on tuera et qui humiliera encore une fois
l'Idée au comble de sa puissance, simplement parce qu'il dira
"non" sans baisser les yeux' (p.115). At this point, it seems to
me, the spectator at Anouilh's play is catapulted out of the
distinctive atmosphere of medieval heresy and witchcraft into
that of twentieth century totalitarian terror, into the grim logic
of the Soviet interrogator in Arthur Koestler's *Darkness at
Noon*. Prayers, faith, errors, visions are eclipsed: all that
remains is the image of dissent tracked down, of persecution and
prisons. In the larger sense, a kind of anachronistic dislocation
has taken place, and it may well be that for Anouilh and those
who share his sympathies in the audience, the figure of
Brasillach stands behind that 'homme à chasser', just as others
will identify him with the Jew deported to the death camps under
Vichy legislation or the resister broken in Gestapo torture-
rooms.

If the figure of the Inquisitor has to be almost portentously
magnified into a kind of horror cartoon in order to allow
Anouilh to make his point about fanaticism and intolerance, in
an admittedly sustained and memorable rhetorical flight, the
Promoter has equally to be wrenched out of his historical
function and reduced to a buffoon so that Anouilh can invite
our contempt and derision for a zealous and time-serving
official who represents a medieval version of the public
prosecutor, precursor of the odious Bitos and those like him
who seek the conviction of ex-collaborators like Brasillach in the
post-war purge trials. Anouilh can derive rather more facile
theatrical effects from some of his other departures from
historical accuracy, such effects being always integrated into a
plausible and consistent, if low and sometimes vulgar, view of
the motivation of certain historical personages. This is the case

with Anouilh's treatment of life at the Dauphin's court. He presents a satirical picture of its emptiness and triviality, reducing it to a round of girlish frivolity over fashionable hats. Here, and in spite of the very broad approach, we recognize that, in feminizing the whole atmosphere of the court, the playwright has found a persuasive device for emphasizing Charles the Dauphin's natural passivity, and a deft way of contrasting a scene of aimless decadence with Joan's robustness, simplicity and sense of mission. Set beside the dramatic effectiveness of such a device, the facts that Agnès Sorel only became Charles's mistress years after the death of Joan of Arc or that Queen Yolande had been dead a year before Charles met Agnès, and was actually politically astute in her support of Charles, seem matters of secondary importance.

Certainly Anouilh's treatment of Charles is in the irreverent Shavian vein, but it is not historically implausible, given what is known about Charles's poor physique, sense of inferiority and general timidity. After all, his mother Isabeau de Bavière had denied his legitimacy, and it is a little excessive to tax Anouilh, as one critic has done, for failing to show in Charles those positive qualities of kingship which he developed only later in life. More suspect, in the sense of soliciting easy laughter, is Anouilh's tendency to infantilize Charles, as when he is shown playing at the child's game of cup-and-ball, though it might be felt even here that the image corresponds well enough with the clichés of national legend and so helps to underline the essentially stylized world of the play. In much the same way, Charles's private confrontation with Joan, first at the court when all the courtiers are obliged to retire and leave them alone, then in the prison at Rouen after Joan has recanted, owe nothing to history but serve powerfully to set her apart from the other actors in the historical events. There is one major inconsistency that springs from such a treatment. In showing Charles as relying entirely on his own impressions and judgement of Joan in their interview at Chinon, Anouilh deliberately discards the historical fact that Joan had been referred to a commission of jurists and theologians who had examined her for a fortnight at Poitiers and reported favourably on her: '... mais en elle on ne trouve point de mal, que bien, humilité, virginité, dévotion, honnêteté, simplesse...' (2, p.11). When Warwick intervenes at the end of this scene, he breaks the stage illusion by reminding us that what we have just seen is at variance with the historical facts about the Theological commission (p.95). In rehandling this situation, Anouilh actually grants to Charles a new stature, a kind of insight, shrewdness and self-confidence that are wholly at odds with the silly and immature prince he has himself invented. Admittedly, there is consistency at another level: the Dauphin's implausibly firm decision does, at least, throw into high relief the force of Joan's personality.

Unlike Shaw, Anouilh follows the historical evidence by granting sympathetic attention to the way in which Joan is worn down through lack of sleep because she has to fend off her guards when they try and molest her. In fact, he deals with this episode much more delicately than Claude Vermorel whose *Jeanne avec nous* (1942) actually enacts (Act III) a coarse scene of near rape where Anouilh is content to have Joan report her difficulties obliquely. Elsewhere Anouilh's inventions serve to create a kind of emotional equilibrium. Having pushed the inhumanity of the Inquisitor and the Promoter to the point of caricature, the dramatist seems to have felt compelled to redress the balance. As a result, Ladvenu, who was not historically Joan's advocate at the trial (an Augustinian monk Isambard de la Pierre occasionally intervened on her behalf), is presented as a deeply humane and concerned cleric whose conduct, along with that of Cauchon, helps to redeem the reputation of the Church. It is to make this point more vividly that Anouilh not only shows him holding up a cross for Joan to see in her last moments at the stake (an action that is historically authentic), but contrasts this with the Promoter's hysterical attempts to deny her this solace, though there is no evidence of any of the clergy present behaving in such a way. Finally, Warwick's role is greatly inflated by Anouilh, as it is by Shaw, from whom Anouilh seems to have borrowed his highly satirical treatment of the duplicitous English gentleman whose exquisite manners conceal the ruthless pursuit of self-interest. In this respect, Claude Vermorel is more faithful to historical fact when he renders Warwick as the brutal and uncomplicated agent of English power, not at all like Anouilh's elegant nobleman gossiping about his fiancée, the hunting field and domestic life at Warwick Castle.

The pervasive sense of anachronism generated by Anouilh's inventions, inflections and distortions of history is, as suggested earlier, reinforced by the play of what I have called 'local' anachronisms. Some of these, as with Cauchon's references, may properly claim to be integrated in the underlying argument about intolerance and the preciousness of the individual conscience with which *L'Alouette* is principally concerned. A riveting example is to be found in Charles's outburst against the horrors of mass democracy, particularly the passage (p.79): 'Des hommes du peuple deviendront les maîtres des royaumes, pour quelques siècles — la durée d'un météore dans le ciel — et ce sera le temps des massacres et des plus monstrueuses erreurs. Et au jour de jugement, quand on fera les additions, on s'apercevra que le plus débauché, le plus capricieux de ses princes aura coûté moins cher au monde, en fin de compte, que l'un de ces hommes vertueux.' For our purpose, it does not matter that such a philosophy of history appears wilfully to minimize the barbarities of earlier periods, or to fail to recognize that régimes have always been as cruel as their means permit. What is important is to note how Charles's allusion to 'ces hommes vertueux' takes him out of his own era, points undisguisedly to Robespierre's 'seagreen Incorruptible' (to borrow from Carlyle), to the Terror's reign of virtue, and beyond that, to the immense and blood-stained tyrannies of modern totalitarian states. Here the voice of poor, feeble Charles is lost in that of his creator, and expresses a horror of mere politics so intense as to verge on anarchism, on the refusal of any kind of political order. It is this horror which, at one level, connects *L'Alouette* and *Pauvre Bitos*, and which will need to be more fully explored in the latter.

Elsewhere Anouilh's local anachronisms in *L'Alouette* offer themselves as purely theatrical devices, embellishments intended to appeal to the complicity of the audience, a complicity which, in recognizing the characteristic 'voice' or persona of the dramatist (his foibles and prejudices) in the anachronisms he

exploits, recognizes at the same time the game-like character of
the enterprise on which he is engaged. In playful anachronism of
this kind Anouilh stands outside his own creation and winks at
the responsive playgoer, who notes appreciatively in passing
how a fifteenth-century monarch can be made to express the
dramatist's (and the public's) dismay over twentieth-century
inflation — 'il y a eu je ne sais combien de dévaluations en
France' (p.77); how Warwick's contempt for a species yet to be
born — 'Ces intellectuels sont ce que je déteste le plus au monde'
(p.130) — is really Anouilh's and their own; and how the
allusions to the prestige of French high fashion (pp.72-73) point
slyly to the bourgeois spectator's own contemporary favourites:
Balmain, Worth, Chanel.

In the broad sense, then, Anouilh's treatment of historical
subject-matter in *L'Alouette* is anachronistic, at variance with
the spirit and values of the epoch he is depicting, though the
nature of these values is, as we shall see, inseparably linked with
the theatrical devices which project them. Anouilh is quite
simply using the fifteenth century to make points he thinks
valuable for the twentieth. The voice that soars over the agents
of political power, theological fanatics, time-serving collaborators, and the lonely victim of *L'Alouette* is a voice appalled by
the cruelties of modern ideological extremism and appealing for
tolerance and forgiveness to a Parisian theatre-going public in
the wake of the post-war political purges. Hence the tone and
temper of *L'Alouette* remain resolutely secular, incurious about
piety or spiritual raptness.

(iii)

In *L'Alouette* Joan is presented both as a touching exemplar
of the stubborn integrity of the individual conscience under
attack and as the supreme symbol of a patriotism that
transcends all divisions within French society. By contrast, Bitos
in *Pauvre Bitos* (the title itself epitomizes contempt and
condescension) exemplifies in his person the tendency of French
society, as Anouilh sees it, to indulge in a perennial civil war of
political factions, with the concomitant and recurring taking of

revenge. As Vulturne puts it (p.63): 'Nous avons tous, de part et d'autre, trop de vilaines histoires derrière nous. Pour longtemps, la haine est française...' History in *Pauvre Bitos* is literally a charade. The characters in the play impersonate leading figures of the French Revolution in a series of episodes which take place in the dreaming mind of the unconscious public prosecutor, Bitos. And, as if to clinch the highly conventionalized nature of the 'history', Anouilh uses one of his characters, Maxime, who functions as a kind of master of ceremonies, to suggest that the historical substance derives from nothing more solid than a history primer popular in French schools: 'Un malheureux comme Julien, qui n'avait jamais pu réussir la première partie de son bachot, pioche son Isaac et Malet depuis quinze jours' (p.34). In fact, the kind of history we are offered relies quite deliberately on a combination of national stereotype and colour-ful anecdote. Predictably, then, we get the Duc de La Rochefoucauld-Liancourt's reply to Louis XVI when the news arrived at Versailles of the fall of the Bastille: 'C'est une révolte? Non, Sire, c'est une révolution' (p.35). Nor does Anouilh stop there. The sensationalism of the moment at the beginning of Act II (p.72), when the prison warder Joseph recalls being drenched with blood from a priest whose skull he has split open with an axe ('Et pourtant, j'avais tapé rude, ça giclait, j'en avais partout...'), not only identifies revolutionary violence with the butcher's shop ('Du boudin de curé') but is plainly intended to express concretely the gross dehumanization of the agents of revolution. It is a brutal and shocking moment which oddly reconciles the demands of stark realism with the convention-alized picture of the Terror one encounters in deeply conservative historical novels like Baroness Orczy's *The Scarlet Pimpernel*. In connecting the excesses of the French Revolution with the political crimes of our own day, Anouilh avoids the elegiac pathos implicit in historical romance by consciously adopting a tone of savage derision.

In an important sense the French Revolution is the creation of historians, its ultimate reality for ever in the process of revision. Hence it would be false to think of some agreed picture of the Revolution from which Anouilh wilfully departs. What can be said of it, as it appears in *Pauvre Bitos*, is that it is quite deliberately partial. In the first place, the Revolution is wholly subsumed in the Terror, seen as an early exercise in totalitarianism. It is about violence, senseless ideological fanaticism, the murderous consequences of a facile and abstract moral rhetoric that fundamentally misconstrues human nature. There is little or nothing in Anouilh's play of the hopes and aspirations of the revolutionaries themselves. The ideals of liberty, civic equality and republican virtue, like the passionate desire to end arbitrary rule and curtail privilege, exist only as ghosts in the interstices of the self-interested conflicts of severely flawed and often unprincipled men. Such idealistic intimations as survive are quickly eclipsed in the welter of blood and corruption. The tally of deaths under the Terror may seem small beer in the light of the reprisals taken against the Paris Communards in May 1871 or the summary executions carried out by rival factions between 1942 and 1945, but they are shown to stem from the same moral causes.

Paradoxically, the device of the charade, performed as a play within a play in the second act, though it distances and even diminishes the Revolution, as I shall try to show in the next chapter, does not wholly destroy the plausibility of Anouilh's own picture of these historical events. By focusing on the Terror and on the power struggle between moderates and extremists, as embodied in a handful of characters, Anouilh actually succeeds in creating the illusion of an impassioned political debate in terms that are not too remote from the rhetorical conventions of the period. As compared with the much freer transposition of characters and their authentic historical roles that we get in *L'Alouette*, *Pauvre Bitos* does not take excessive liberties with the personalities and political views of the main protagonists. Of course, it is true that set beside the more nuanced picture offered by modern historical research, Anouilh exaggerates to the point of caricature certain qualities in his leading politicians — Danton's emotionalism and horseplay, for example, or the neurotic tics that are visited on Robespierre — and seems here to be responding to national folklore rather than to any impulse to understand these figures. In addition, he creates a quite consistent sense of the political ambience of the period through deft, rapid and selective references to debates in the Convention, Hébert's scurrilous newspaper *Le Père Duchesne*, the laws of the maximum which controlled prices, and the law of 22 prairial (10 June 1794) which extended the Revolutionary Tribunal's powers of summary justice. Such specific details, judiciously scattered through the speeches, generate the illusion of historical depth and suggest an authentic reading of the period.

This illusion of authenticity is supported by the infrequency and discretion with which Anouilh departs from known facts. There are trivial inaccuracies of dating (over Robespierre's maiden speech or Tallien's marriage to the widowed Marquise de Fontenay), and some telescoping of chronology, as when we move from a scene involving Mirabeau, who died in April 1791, to one which refers to an article in Camille Desmoulin's *Le Vieux Cordelier*, which cannot be earlier than March 1794. Such a shift appears to reflect the playwright's determination to accelerate the momentum of the action. In presenting Robespierre as being shot in the jaw by the gendarme Merda (usually referred to as 'Méda') Anouilh tends not to follow the consensus of modern historians. The result is slyly to diminish Robespierre, implying that for all his cult of antiquity, the Incorruptible lacked the 'Roman' courage to attempt suicide.

So *Pauvre Bitos* accumulates the incidentals of the Revolutionary period more conscientiously and contrives a more plausible historical surface than *L'Alouette*, but, like the latter, it is not really concerned with historical reconstruction. The vivacity of the reactions of the Parisian theatre critics confirms the play's essentially anachronistic character. In this respect, the judgement of the Communist Party newspaper, *L'Humanité*, is not unrepresentative of the outrage provoked generally by the play in left-wing circles: 'M. Anouilh a voulu dire sa haine du communisme, bien entendu, et de la Résistance, sa haine de la démocratie, sa haine de la Révolution de 89, etc...'.[5] This clearly interprets *Pauvre Bitos* as appealing to the France of 1956 over the heads of its eighteenth-century invented characters, and as offering the Terror as a paradigm of the excesses of

[5] *L'Humanité*, 13 October 1956, quoted in Comminges (*12*, p.85).

Communism, of the Resistance insofar as that can be identified with the Communist Party, and ultimately of mass democracy itself. The partisan fury that enters into these reactions must be explained in part by the political context of the time, by the pressures of the Suez crisis and the Algerian War which polarized French opinion, setting Right against Left in a spirit of intense bitterness.

But such reactions have also to be explained in terms of the particular character and thrust of Anouilh's theatrical transposition of history. Unlike *L'Alouette*, which presents a single world of the past where local anachronisms disconcert and stimulate the spectator by abruptly importing the twentieth century into the medieval world of the play, *Pauvre Bitos* moves through two discrete, though intimately connected, worlds. The first is resolutely that of the twentieth century and is filled out with references to petrol stations and night clubs, apart from topical allusions to politics. The second is that of the Terror and is studded with anachronisms which serve deliberately to link the conflicts of the Revolution with those of France after 1945. When Saint-Just, in the dream-play of Act II, sardonically applauds Robespierre's proposals for the law of 22 prairial, the Parisian public of the twentieth century instantly recognizes that his references to the retroactive legislation of the Terror are meant to apply to the same phenomenon as it operates in the post-war trials in France: 'Effet rétroactif. Jurés partisans. Pas de défense. C'est un modèle du genre. Il resservira...' (p.102). And when, in the same scene (p.103), Robespierre effectively signs the death warrant of the poet André Chénier ('Chénier n'est pas un poète. C'est un contre-révolutionnaire!'), the audience at the first night of the play would have needed no prompting to see in this an allusion to the execution of Brasillach by a vengeful and triumphant coalition of the Left. Indeed, given that Chénier is shown to be the victim of a fanatical revolutionary cabal, his death is almost certainly intended to symbolize that of Brasillach. Such a parallel conveniently over-looks Brasillach's own political fanaticism and virulent anti-semitism, not to say the executions of Communist intellectuals like Gabriel Péri by fanatics of a different persuasion with whom Brasillach sympathized. However, it confirms the degree to which the presence of the dead Brasillach haunts *Pauvre Bitos*. His ghost is conjured up again in the gross and racy cynicism of Brassac, in the twentieth-century setting of Act III, when he replies to Bitos: '... En France, on trouve toujours un général pour signer un décret ou pour refuser une grâce...' (p.116). This savage gibe at the expense of de Gaulle, who had declined to pardon Brasillach, would have struck a sympathetic chord in the ex-collaborators in the theatre, while infuriating the ex-resisters for whom the invocation of the trials would serve to diminish their sacrifices and achievements to the level of a squalid vendetta.

It seems a little disingenuous to interpret these allusions as attacks on fanaticism and abuse of power which succeed in transcending mere party. The victims for whom the spectators' sympathies are elicited are invariably victims of the ruthless violence of the Left. In purely theatrical terms, it is the terrorism of the Left which is graphically embodied in blood-thirsty individuals (Robespierre, Saint-Just, even the warder Joseph, Anouilh's version of the common man), and which is enacted on stage in a series of violent speeches and decisions. Terrorism of the Right (the murders of the Thermidorian reaction, the White Terror of the Midi conducted against the supporters of Napoleon in 1815) is nowhere *embodied* in the inner play of *Pauvre Bitos*, but simply conceded verbally (Act III, pp.115-16) by a spuriously jovial Brassac in a scene of drunken euphoria which effectively neutralizes the value of the admissions being made: '... En fait, nous ne vous reprochons rien du tout. Nous ne sommes pas des enfants! Les exécutions sommaires c'est comme les boules, c'est un jeu français. Chez nous, on sait ça en naissant.' In a word, if one is attentive to the effects produced by the action of the play itself, one is soon made aware that Anouilh's image of the Terror functions very imperfectly as a device for condemning *alr* forms of political fanaticism. What it tends to do is to associate violent excess with the activities and ideology of a quasi-Communist régime. A crucial anachronism of the play within a play in Act II conduces, in an analogous way, to discredit the Resistance by associating it with cheap opportunists who join its ranks at the last moment. Such is the effect which is produced (p.73) when the time-serving prison warder, Charles, uses the neologism 'bastillards' (with its echoes of 'maquisards') to dismiss those who acquired fraudulent certificates attesting to their having participated in the storming of the Bastille: 'Remarque que tout le monde ne pouvait pas y être. Ça aurait fait de l'encombrement. Ça aurait plutôt gêné. Mais j'en connais qui se sont fait faire de faux certificats comme quoi, ils y étaient. Et à eux les bonnes places! Il y a eu un temps où il n'y en avait que pour les bastillards.' This is a good, and characteristically ferocious, Anouilh joke, for it is perfectly true that numerous opportunists did in fact join the Resistance in the final months of the German Occupation and subsequently secured advantages from doing so. However, the significance of this sally comes from the way in which it adds to the cumulative effect of presenting the Resistance, at least by implication, as largely concerned with venality and revenge. Nor can it be said that such a picture (which ignores so much) is offset by a persuasive alternative vision of the Resistance. It has to be admitted that the figure of the idealistic young schoolmaster, Deschamps, is introduced in order to lend the Resistance a reputable and human face, just as his *alter ego*, Camille Desmoulins, is produced so as to incarnate an acceptable revolutionary idealism. But Deschamps remains a wan and marginal character, is given little to say, and is overwhelmed by the social poise and implacable self-interest of his 'betters', just as Camille is quite overshadowed by Robespierre and Saint-Just. Only once, in an audacious allusion, does Anouilh seem to me to touch on the victims of terror in terms that can be made to accommodate figuratively not only the crimes of communism but the horrors of fascism and the death camps. It is that chilling moment when the warder Joseph's narrative of the tumbrils flatly and disconcertingly conjures up the practice of the guards at Auschwitz as they shepherded Jews into the gas-chambers: 'On leur disait de prendre leurs affaires, ça leur donnait confiance et on les faisait passer un à un dans la cour où nous, on les attendait et hop!...' (p.72).

In choosing the historical subjects of Joan of Arc and

Robespierre, Anouilh has imaginatively found a way of dealing with the conflicting political ideologies of his own time (notably as crystallized under the German Occupation) and his personal relationship to them. However, he does this not simply by altering and rearranging the historical record and inventing details of his own, but by locating this reworked historical material within the imagined, self-consistent and autonomous world which he conjures up in all his plays. In this sense, history undergoes a double transformation at Anouilh's hands: he uses parts of the historical record, alters and inflects them in quite specific ways, and then reorders them according to the distinctive conventions, patterns and types that mark his theatre as a whole. In short, history functions as part of an aesthetic continuum that can be conveniently epitomized in a single dominant metaphor: the world is a stage.

2. The Metaphor of the Stage

(i)

It is true that much that is innovatory in the modern European theatre derives its power and fascination from the self-conscious way in which the resources of pure theatricality are exploited, but no modern playwright, with the exception of Pirandello, has outdone Anouilh in assimilating moral and emotional experience to the traditional types and conventions of the stage. No dramatist of this century has more fully identified human life with the life of the stage or more consciously embodied in his plays Shakespeare's great image:

> All the world's a stage,
> And all the men and women merely players:
> They have their exits and their entrances...

Whether Anouilh's own handling of this metaphor in *L'Alouette* and *Pauvre Bitos* affords us commanding insights into human experience or whether it simply represents an arresting but glib scenic convention, is something I shall return to. First, it will be useful to look, in a rapid and summary way, at how this central metaphor of the world as a stage is articulated throughout the whole range of Anouilh's drama before exploring precisely how it works in the two plays we are dealing with.

From Anouilh's earliest plays to his latest, the presence of theatrical metaphors as a way of expressing human experience is so dense and pervasive as to constitute a closed world of echo, association and allusion. And this impression of artifice and enclosure is reinforced by a great variety of devices, all inducing in the spectator the conviction that he is viewing not some form of common reality but an elevated game which belongs uniquely to the realm of theatrical representation. Some of these devices are peculiarly effective in suggesting the degree to which Anouilh's stage world becomes parasitic on itself and on the literary and dramatic traditions on which it draws.

There is the device of the recurring character, like the figure of the harassed or misunderstood playwright, called Antoine or Antonio, who is the author's persona and who surfaces in slightly different guises in *Episode de la vie d'un auteur* (1948), *Cher Antoine ou l'amour raté* (1969), *Les Poissons rouges* (1970), and *Le Directeur de l'opéra* (1972). Such a device is further complicated when Carlotta, the playwright's first wife in *Cher Antoine*, is presented as engaged in a kind of perpetual play-acting which echoes the antics of an earlier actress created by Anouilh, the posturing Madame Alexandra of *Colombe* (1951), who remorselessly carries over her stage roles into her everyday life. This impression of an artificial and self-contained world is revived through Anouilh's tongue-in-cheek use of names for minor characters that blatantly recall English classics of the stage or novel — Shakespeare's Juliet and Capulet, Richardson's Lovelace and Pamela — and which import into his own dramatic situations a touch of the operatic, a whiff of high tragic passion quite at variance with their actual banality. Similar effects are produced in *La Répétition ou l'amour puni* (1950), itself a kind of pastiche of an eighteenth-century comedy, by Anouilh's knowing allusions to stock French plays of the nineteenth century, such as Dumas *fils*'s *La Dame aux camélias* and Scribe's *Adrienne Lecouvreur*. Even more striking is Anouilh's recourse to wilful and artfully contrived plagiarism, as in *Cher Antoine* when the Bavarian castle is boarded up and the blows of the carpenter's hammer audaciously echo the strokes of the axe so hauntingly familiar from the ending of Chekov's *The Cherry Orchard*. In a word, we are almost never allowed to see the world except in terms of the life of the stage. Even Anouilh's sets tend to be highly stagey and pictorial: an actual theatre or opera-house (*Colombe*, *Le Directeur de l'opéra*), a country mansion whose public rooms easily accommodate private theatricals (*La Répétition*), or a stately home that has actually been converted into a huge peep-show

(La Belle Vie, 1979). Elsewhere the set takes the form of a construction so grandiose and elaborate that it strikes one, in the figurative sense, as theatrical: the baroque castle of Cher Antoine or the great vaulting conservatory of L'Invitation au château (1947).

If theatricality is not in the grand design, it is to be found in the colour and stylish formality of the costumes in those plays situated in Anouilh's preferred period, the eighteen nineties (La Valse des toréadors, 1952); if not there, in the sort of spectacle provided by the fancy-dress ball in Le Bal des voleurs (1938). Such theatricality is even more piquantly available to us in the professional entertainers who throng the plays: the desperate Thérèse who belongs to a precarious palm-court orchestra in La Sauvage (1938), or Mme de Montalembreuse, an actress who specializes in playing dignified mothers in Le Rendez-vous de Senlis (1941), or Orphée reborn as a kind of street busker in Eurydice (1942). When Anouilh is not confronting us with professional actors, he presents us with characters who are either putting on an act or so completely lost in stylized roles that we can associate them only with life behind the footlights. As examples of the latter, one thinks of the stately identical butlers who glide through Léocadia (1940), and of the Duchess in L'Hermine (1932) and Lady Hurf in Le Bal des voleurs, two fantasticated survivors of a vanished era whose pedigree is no more real than that of Oscar Wilde's imperious Lady Bracknell in The Importance of Being Earnest.

The apparently ceaseless desire to impersonate, to perform roles before others, marks not only historical figures, like Napoleon, but encroaches on the very heart of privacy, on the life of families. It is there in the relations between father and daughter in Cécile ou l'école des pères (1954): 'Parce que je suis votre père et que vous êtes ma fille, nous nous croyons obligés l'un et l'autre de jouer des rôles tout faits' (PB, p.507). It is present in the hectic succession of roles played out in dream or fantasy by the eternally quarrelling ménage in Le Boulanger, la boulangère et le petit mitron (1968) and which include story-book impersonations of members of the French royal family on the eve of the Revolution. As for the Napoleon of La Foire *d'empoigne*, he is presented as a cheap public performer armed with empty gestures and rhetorical tricks learned from the great tragedian Talma. Like a popular actor who has become identified with certain parts, he must persist in playing the character ('le petit caporal') the public expects of him, a view he reveals to be perfectly consistent with his conception of history: 'Mon petit ami, nous ne sommes pas au théâtre. Ou plutôt, si, nous y sommes...mais pas dans la tragédie, dans le mélo, comme au boulevard du Temple. Moi, je suis un acteur de drame historique...' (*PC*, p.323). And this confident formula, which seems to reduce history to a charade, simply echoes what is said earlier in Anouilh's career by that Monsieur Henri, who may be death in disguise, and who serves as a one-man chorus in *Eurydice*: 'Cette pitrerie, ce mélo absurde, c'est la vie. Cette lourdeur, ces effets de théâtre, c'est bien elle' (*PN*, pp.500-01).

So complete an assimilation of life to the conventions of the stage finds further expression in Anouilh's regular and parodistic use of certain dramatic modes, notably melodrama and farce. The resources of bedroom farce, a favourite genre of the Belle Epoque public, are repeatedly, and sometimes wearisomely, exploited. There pass before our eyes a long procession of cuckolds, lecherous old men, elderly coquettes, long-suffering maids, jealous wives and imperious mistresses. Nowhere are they more wildly absurd than in *La Valse des toréadors* where General Saint-Pé's deceived wife threatens to die spectacularly for love, choosing a railway crossing at which no train is expected for twenty four hours; or *Le Boulanger, la boulangère et le petit mitron* where Adolphe and Elodie move frantically in imagination from one adulterous tryst to another. In a comparable way, two early plays, *L'Hermine* (1932) and *Jézabel* (written 1932), concentrate the themes, conventions and properties of melodrama to an extreme degree, though here, as with Anouilh's farces, the result is to infiltrate them with a curious and haunting sense of moral anguish and despair. However, the high density of melodramatic effects confirms the parodistic tendencies in these two plays: a brutal murder, idiot servant, police interrogation and last-minute confession in *L'Hermine*; a drunken nymphomaniac, poisoned mushrooms,

and a blackmailing maid in *Jézabel*. Nor does Anouilh entirely
discard the cruder stage conventions later in his career, as one
can judge from *Cher Antoine*, where the castle is cut off by
snow, a howling dog mourns its deceased master, and the dead
playwright's voice comes floating out of the gramophone.

In some respects, the most compelling use of the theatrical
metaphor is to be found in Anouilh's handling of the device of
the play within a play. It is already present in the skilful way in
which prologue and chorus frame the inner play between
Antigone and Créon in *Antigone* (1944), but is subsequently
developed more elaborately in a number of plays, including
L'Alouette and *Pauvre Bitos*, to which we shall return. For
example, *Le Boulanger, la boulangère et le petit mitron* is
structured about a whole sequence of inset dream-scenes or
fantasy projections which transpose in graphic form the
frustrations, failures and discontents of the ill-assorted couple,
Antoine and Elodie. In *Le Directeur de l'opéra* this device takes
the form of an improvised nativity play, in *La Belle Vie* that of
the public performances which the displaced aristocratic family
has to provide for the new revolutionary audience. Most
ambitious of all is the sustained use of the play within a play in
La Répétition where Anouilh moves, with exhilarating deftness
and confidence, between the text of his own play and that of
Marivaux's *La Double inconstance*, which is being rehearsed by
Anouilh's invented characters (the Comte and his friends), and
between the on-stage spectators of the Marivaux comedy in
rehearsal and the real-life spectators of his own play in
performance.

In the light of this theatrical practice, what kinds of significance are we to attach to the dominant imagery of the stage in
Anouilh's plays? First, it should be said that such images, while
reinforcing our sense of a strikingly autonomous imaginary
world, also run the risk of creating a narrowly repetitive one.
This narrowness hardly matters in the case of some of Anouilh's
early *pièces roses*, light-hearted plays like *Le Bal des voleurs*,
Léocadia and *L'Invitation au château*, where the ubiquitous
figures of impersonation and stage representation are perfectly
matched to the exuberant fancy of comedies in which all comes

right in the end, in a spirit of festive make-believe. However, such self-conscious borrowing from the traditional conventions and stereotypes of the stage, when applied to plays that embody moral and emotional intensity (Thérèse's almost religious feeling for poverty in *La Sauvage* or Joan's despair at being abandoned in *L'Alouette*), epitomizes a kind of aesthetic impasse. It is as if Anouilh were signalling to us that genuine tragedy is foreign to the temper of our age, that the tragic world-view implies reconciliation with some over-arching moral order, however imperfectly grasped or assented to, that our prevailing scepticism and unbelief cannot provide such an order, and that consequently no agreed and satisfactory convention now exists for expressing tragic experience on the stage. In this sense, recourse to highly conventionalized dramatic forms that radically simplify the complexity of moral experiences and the variety of human types may represent a kind of nostalgia on Anouilh's part for a stable but vanished moral and social order. Certainly Anouilh possesses a distinctive moral perspective in his plays, and whatever coherence we grant it tends to derive from the persuasiveness with which he uses imagery drawn from the traditional life of the stage in order to articulate it. Identifying that moral vision in the busy traffic of game, illusion and artifice of which his plays are composed, is the challenge which the play-goer faces in Anouilh's plays. Unquestionably a vivid stage activity is paraded before us in *L'Alouette* and *Pauvre Bitos*, and we now need to scrutinize precisely how the devices of impersonation and performance operate in these two plays, how they distance Anouilh's chosen themes — Joan's faith and integrity under duress, the inhumanity of political fanaticism — and affect his treatment of myth and time, characterization, and dramatic language.

(ii)

The exploitation of traditional stage conventions and of imagery drawn from the practice of the stage is inseparable, in both *L'Alouette* and *Pauvre Bitos*, from Anouilh's handling of myth and time. In choosing the trial and burning of Joan of Arc

and the culmination of the Terror and Robespierre's execution
as the subject matter of his plays, Anouilh is necessarily con-
strained to adopt the order of the historical narrative he has
inherited. From the outset we know that Joan and Robespierre
have to die and that the dramatist is not free to invent another
end for them, as he would be had he chosen to present us with
purely fictive characters. In this limited respect, it might be
argued that a playwright who follows the order of the original
myth condemns himself to an art of embellishment, at least as
compared with the dramatist who invents a 'myth' that draws on
the materials of contemporary experience immediately available
to him in order to make a statement of large human significance
that transcends the present age while yet addressing it. Sartre's
Les Séquestrés d'Altona might be thought to use the fate of a
Nazi war criminal in just such a way so as to raise issues about
freedom, moral responsibility and guilt. In the context of
L'Alouette and *Pauvre Bitos*, Anouilh's creative freedom lies in
interpreting the character of historical personages and in
departing from the original time-sequence he finds in the
historical record. In the first case, the result is (as we shall see
later) to remove the protagonists from their historical setting
and to assimilate them to the family of characters he has made
us familiar with in his other plays. In the second case, the
consequence is to dislocate the sense of the past, to divest
recorded episodes from the past of their historical specificity, to
make them timeless, in the sense of belonging to no time and to
all time (including our own), and so radically to alter their
significance as myths.

Hence, while Shaw adheres strictly to the chronological order
of Joan's life and trial, Anouilh, in *L'Alouette*, invents his own
significant order by abandoning that scheme and presenting
Joan's life and trial in the form of 'plays within plays', set
within the unfolding evidence of the trial and bearing all the
marks of a ritual reenactment. In doing so, he annuls both time
and space, the former by allowing us to move freely back and
forth in time, notably when the final coronation scene reverses
the order of events already provided for in the inset dramatized
scenes, and the latter by confronting us with a rapid succession

of episodes played out in a purely conventional space and improvised from the stage properties and costumes that happen to be lying around, in such a way as to represent Joan at home or in a corner of a battlefield or at the Dauphin's court. The dramatic structure of the action in this play, lacking both formal acts and scenes, powerfully enhances the sense of fluidity and, as a consequence, blurs our notion of time. In a comparable way, though *Pauvre Bitos* is laid out in three acts, the introduction of characters in Act I who are wearing historical 'heads' while clearly living in our present-day world, the creation of a dream eighteenth century in Act II in which they continue to be present, and the abrupt return to the twentieth century in Act III, all help to keep the spectator in a state of temporal confusion and uncertainty.

This playing with time only works because it forms an integral part of a whole series of conventions available to us in the plays, all emphasizing impersonation, performance and theatrical illusion. (I have deferred to the next chapter my scrutiny of Anouilh's persistent use of self-quotation from his earlier plays, since this device relates principally to his handling of character.) In neither of these two plays is any attempt made to persuade us that what we are witnessing is 'real'; on the contrary, we are constantly invited to recognize the traffic of the stage as patently illusory, as something contrived so as to create vivid immediacy. The opening stage directions of *L'Alouette* already make clear that we are embarking on a kind of game. What we are about to see has been performed before, since, as the actors come on, they take up those properties or articles of clothing that have been left on stage since the previous performance: '*En entrant, les personnages décrochent leurs casques ou certains de leurs accessoires qui avaient été laissés sur scène à la fin de la précédente représentation, ils s'installent sur les bancs dont ils rectifient l'ordonnance*' (p.41). This notion of reenactment is reinforced by our first meeting with Warwick who is not initially presented as an historical agent but as a sort of stage director anxious to begin immediately with the trial scene. He is opposed by Cauchon who wants the whole story to be enacted again: 'Domrémy, les Voix, Vaucouleurs, Chinon, le Sacre...' (p.41).

In insisting politely that Joan's life was so short that it would not take long to reenact the whole of it, Cauchon makes plain to us as spectators that what is proposed is quite simply a ritual reenactment of something which is already over, already passed into history. And the conventional or game-like character of what he suggests is emphasized when he genially concedes to Warwick that they can skip the battles: '...nous ne sommes pas assez nombreux pour jouer les batailles...' (p.42). So the stage performance of Anouilh's play which has been set in motion (pp.41-42) now leads to the performance of the inner play about Joan's life (pp.42-46).

Joan begins, and the actors who are not immediately required move into the unlit or dimly lit areas of the stage as Joan's mother, father and brother move into the light of centre stage. Even at this moment, the idea of mere performance is plainly restated when someone off asks who will perform the Voices. Joan insists it must be her and begins the narrative of her life, having been assured that she can start where she pleases (p.42). Her account of her early experience of the Voices and of her first encounter with St Michael is interrupted by Warwick, encouraged by Cauchon, then disrupted by the intervention of Beaudricourt (who has mistaken his cue) before continuing. These interruptions powerfully underline the fact that we are witnessing a simple performance, and they subvert our possible emotional identification with Joan's mystical experience and initial terrors, just as the fact of her impersonating the Voices reinforces our sense that something is being acted out, not experienced directly. There follows (pp.45-46) the first of Joan's inset scenes with her family (depicting her father's violent anger, her mother's concern and her brother's malice) before there is a further interruption, this time by the Promoter, the effect of which is to undercut the realism of the father's rage and to remind us that it is all a game. Even the Promoter's growing vehemence at this point (pp.45-50), as he presses his theological charges, has its reality seriously undermined when he makes a fool of himself by unconsciously unmasking his own lubricious fantasies as he talks of the Devil: 'Il prend les traits d'une belle fille toute nue, les seins dressés, insupportablement belle...'

(p.48). His fanaticism and the solemnity of his public function dissolve in the actors' and spectators' knowing sniggers, and this effect of almost Brechtian distancing is strengthened when Cauchon intervenes (p.48) to remind the Promoter that they have not yet reached the trial. There are further interventions by the Inquisitor (is Joan in a state of grace?) and by Ladvenu, both tending to intensify the theological gravity of Joan's position, but even here the Maid's self-consciousness about being involved in a performance which is going awry, breaks through: 'On ne sait plus où on en est. On mélange tout' (p.50). She is thoroughly confused as to whether they are talking about her Voices or about the end of the trial when she becomes aware of being deserted by her king and companions in arms.

At this point, Warwick intervenes to protest at their slowness in getting to the trial and to reveal his own confusion over the chronology of events (pp.51-52). This leads to the scene of Joan being beaten by her father (pp.52-55), a scene reenacted with such brutal vigour that Ladvenu is moved to interfere, only to be checked by Cauchon who observes that they can do nothing to alter the past: 'Nous ne pouvons que jouer nos rôles, chacun le sien, bon ou mauvais, tel qu'il est écrit, et à son tour' (p.55). Nothing could more appropriately epitomize the importance accorded to the metaphor of the stage in this play. In effect, Joan's life is presented as a ritual that can neither be altered nor arrested. When Cauchon and Warwick comment on the episode in which Joan is beaten, they do so with the detachment of figures in a chorus. The scene of family life resumes (pp.53-58), revealing the parents' incomprehension of Joan's behaviour, before merging with another (pp.58-60) in which Joan, like some medium in trance, articulates the message of St Michael, failing to realise that the stern rebuke 'Orgueilleuse!' has come from her own mouth (p.59). This arresting moment, when a purely vocal effect dominates the empty stage, characteristically extends Anouilh's use of theatrical metaphor by making Joan a sort of ventriloquist's puppet responding to supernatural voices. Yet even this deeply moving incident, which enables Joan to express her fears about the burden of sanctity and her divine mission, is not handled so as to win us over to a full sympathetic

identification with her plight. Abruptly Joan reverts to childhood, as the stage directions make clear: '... *soudain elle
redevient une petite fille et s'exclame joyeuse et décidée, se
tapant sur la cuisse...*' (p.60). The effect is to remind us vividly
that we are merely witnessing a performance, and that is enough
to check our nascent temptation to enter imaginatively into the
doubt, loneliness and suffering of Joan's life. Such a reaction is
all the more emphatic since the return to childhood is conveyed
(p.60) by a rough brawl between Joan and her brother,
accompanied by a torrent of childish abuse ('vermine', 'petit
cochon', 'sale bête').

In a comparable way, the scene between Joan and
Beaudricourt which follows (pp.60-69) not only enacts an
episode in Joan's past life as if it were happening in the stage
characters' present (a feature of all these inset plays), but has its
illusion of reality almost instantly neutralized when it is
commented on in a detached and condescending way by
Warwick and Cauchon (pp.69-72). Cauchon's own remarks
persistently imply that the trial and burning are in the past, and
at least one of his comments is important not only for the kind
of argument which it advances in favour of Joan's lonely
intransigence, but for the way in which the phrasing of the
argument consciously anticipates part of the Inquisitor's later
speech (pp.114-15), offers itself as the counterpart of that
speech, and so establishes an effect of symmetry which throws
into relief Anouilh's dominant concern for the formal ordering
of *L'Alouette*. I am thinking specifically of the way in which
Cauchon's 'Mais c'est dans cette solitude, dans ce silence d'un
Dieu disparu, dans ce dénuement et cette misère de bête, que
l'homme qui continue à redresser la tête est bien grand' (p.71)
prefigures and counters the Inquisitor's outraged condemnation
of rebellious man: 'Il se retourne, il fait face sous la torture, sous
l'humiliation et les coups, dans cette misère de bête, sur la litière
humide de son cachot; il lève les yeux vers cette image invaincue
de lui-même...' (p.114).

All this self-conscious exploitation of theatricalist devices is
repeated in the scene at the Court (pp.72-95), the longest
continuous episode in the entire play, since the lengthy scene of

the trial is interrupted by the intervention of La Hire (pp.109-12). This not only suggests the degree of dramatic detail which Anouilh lavishes on Joan's scenes with the Dauphin, in a manner reminiscent of Shaw, but establishes a slowing down of the dramatic tempo which effectively grants the spectator a respite before he is caught up in the remorseless momentum of the last phase of the trial. The episode at Chinon is formally presented by Warwick in his role as stage director ('Mais écoutons plutôt Chinon, Monseigneur'), and the stage directions clearly indicate that we are not going to be confronted with the illusion of life, but with a rather hastily improvised performance: '*Il se tourne vers les gens de Chinon qui ont occupé le plateau, dressant avec les moyens du bord une petite mise en scène du palais, pendant qu'ils bavardaient*' (p.72). Similarly, the scene ends with a tableau when Joan, the Dauphin and the courtiers are 'frozen' in at attitude of prayer as the Archbishop gives his benediction (p.95). What follows reinforces even more strikingly the sense we as spectators have of watching an elaborate charade. As the stage directions prescribe: '*Le rideau tombe sur le tableau vivant de la bénédiction; quand il se relève sur la seconde partie de la pièce, l'Archevêque est toujours en train de bénir Charles et Jeanne, mais tous les autres acteurs sont revenus sur scène autour d'eux et Warwick enchaîne*' (p.95).

At this point, Warwick elegantly and ironically summarizes Joan's victories in the field and her capture at Compiègne. This piece of narration, which effectively opens the second part of the play, contrasts sharply with the already established convention of deploying inset scenes which vividly enact chosen moments in Joan's life. It reinforces our sense that the playwright remains self-consciously attentive to dramatic symmetry since it echoes the only other piece of narrative summary featured in the play: the moment near the beginning of the first part (p.43) in which Joan narrates the circumstances leading up to her earliest visions before reenacting her past for our benefit. In a very similar way, Warwick's narration (pp.95-96) leads into the reenactment of Joan's experiences, starting with a piece of mime (p.96) in which Charles and the court slink away, abandoning Joan who is still lost in prayer. This miming constitutes a brilliantly elliptical device for effecting the shift from a Joan who has won the trust of her sovereign and is confident of her God-given mission, to the deserted heretic whose trial is now to be played out before us. At the most intense moments of this trial, the participants are still shown as coming forward on cue, while even the menacing and implacable fury of the Inquisitor, which threatens to draw us as spectators into the living ordeal of the trial by touching off our emotional identification with the vulnerable Joan, is actually short-circuited by the rough and bawdy intervention of La Hire (pp.109-12). He is picked out in a spotlight as the rest of the cast recede into the shadows, and leaves the stage vigorously miming an attack on the English in a way which confirms the essentially unreal or play-acting nature of what we see in front of us.

Metaphors drawn from the life of the stage and devices of self-conscious theatricality are notably subdued in the rest of the trial scene (pp.112-26), when Joan recants and is condemned to perpetual imprisonment, as in the immediate aftermath of the trial, when there is cynical relief in official circles at her decision. Nor are they any more in evidence in the prison scene (pp.128-33) when Joan relapses and recovers her sense of divine mission. However, such imagery and devices return with renewed force once Joan has called for her male clothes and summoned the clergy to witness her change of heart. The tempo of the action suddenly accelerates. Everything is rapid, furtive, improvised, 'like a murder' or a 'police raid', as the stage directions insist, emphasizing the stylized nature of the movements. The rest of the cast come on stage ahead of Joan and the executioner. It is they who, breaking through any residual illusion of realism, bring faggots for the burning and help to erect a makeshift pyre from the planks that have served as seats for the trial. And this developed sense of conventionality, which maintains us in a state of alert detachment, is reinforced when the crowd shouts 'Au poteau! Tondez-la, la fille à soldats' (p.133), in an allusion which audaciously lifts the spectators out of the fifteenth century and recalls them to the Paris of August 1944 where prostitutes and other female 'collaborators' with the Germans have their heads shaved. Finally, and most crucially, at

the moment when Joan is about to expire, Beaudricourt charges
on, complaining that, in enacting Joan's past, the crowd has
overlooked the coronation at Rheims, the supreme triumph of
her life. The pyre is hastily dismantled, an altar raised, and the
coronation reenacted with all pomp and colour so that the
curtain falls on a graphically impressive tableau in which Joan is
petrified for ever in the conventional posture of illustrated
history books: '*Le rideau tombe lentement sur cette belle image
de livre de prix...*' (p.137). This clinching image emerges not as
one of a series of purely local effects, but as part of a consistent
and recurring way of viewing human experience that vitally
affects the significance we as spectators are prepared to grant to
that experience. Beginnings and endings are, of course,
peculiarly important in the ordering of literary forms, and it
needs to be said that this vivid impression of a coronation at the
end of *L'Alouette* subsumes in a single crowning image the
whole tendency of the play, from Warwick's first entry
onwards, to offer itself as an elaborate theatrical game.
Everything in the play must be seen as leading to that end, and
the end must be seen as determining the significance of what has
gone before.

Joan literally acts out her life, stepping from the 'present' of
the ecclesiastical court into the 'past' and 'future' of the scenes
she reenacts. In doing so, she moves through what Pronko calls
the 'timeless light of the stage' (*26*, p.157). The outer play,
which Warwick and Cauchon set in motion, and which Warwick
controls in his role as master of ceremonies, effectively frames
the inner play (the vivid and concrete inset scenes) and distances
us from it. We may be caught up in the passions and conflicts of
the inner play while they are actually being reenacted, but the
intermittent commentary of Warwick or Cauchon and the open
deployment of scenic effects, with characters acting on cue and
helping to arrange the set, provide us with sharp breaks from the
illusion of life generated by the inset scenes, and so offer us a
detached perspective on such scenes. The result is to involve
intelligence more than feeling: we are always conscious of
watching a play in which life, like time itself, is being mani-
pulated. A curious ambiguity arises from this technique. The

device of having Joan reenact her life before our eyes
strengthens our sense of the fatality inherent in the play and, at
moments, evokes the ghost of tragic inevitability. But
Warwick's ironic comments and masterful interference with the
progress of the play, the radical dislocation of the time scheme,
and the undisguised presentation of characters as actors in a
repeat performance, all work against this potential tragic sense
and even subvert it. This sort of technique is presumably what
prompts Howarth (*19*, p.278) to describe Anouilh as a
'demythologiser', a playwright who voids myth and legend of
their metaphysical implications.

The breakdown of the traditional legend which we find in
L'Alouette might be said to be reflected in the sense of strain
and incoherence we experience when scenes of low comedy are
juxtaposed to scenes of high seriousness. One thinks of the
broad, and often coarse, effects which Anouilh draws from the
extended scenes which he devotes to Joan being beaten by her
clownish father, or brazenly flattering Beaudricourt, or revelling
in La Hire's animal appetites. All these tend to displace Joan's
religious vision from the centre of the play and to exaggerate her
ordinariness and common humanity. In this way she is certainly
rescued from the pious sentimentality of official hagiography,
but it is not easy to reconcile this figure of Joan with the
ingenuous girl who believes herself, however mistakenly, to be
the vessel of God. Yet, given the extreme knowingness with
which the play is handled, we have to accept this as a calculated
effect intended by Anouilh to subvert the public's idealized
image of Joan. Such an effect is consistent with the general tenor
of the play, which is to secularize Joan, to show her as a
stubborn individual conscience pitted against established
authority and orthodoxy rather than as a visionary touched by
the divine. For Anouilh, Joan's preciousness, and the meaning
of her suffering, come from her being true to herself, from her
heroic integrity and commitment, against all odds. He is not
primarily interested in her as the embodiment of religious faith
and piety, nor even as the midwife of French nationhood. These
are simply ways in which her extraordinary personal adventure
has become institutionalized; they cannot account for the

phenomenon Joan was. Only her peculiar moral intransigence can do that, and it is precisely that intransigence which, Anouilh seems to be saying, needs to be celebrated, memorialized, and rescued from the accretions of national legend. This seems to me the key to understanding how the final coronation scene works theatrically.

By reversing the normal order of events at the very moment of the burning, Anouilh reinforces in the mind of his audience the idea that they have witnessed not some tragic and exemplary passion in which they were sympathetically involved, but the adroit manipulation of a series of theatrical illusions. The conflict between the logic of the coronation scene (the triumph of Joan in the secular world) and the logic of earlier scenes which represent Joan's triumph as spiritual — as when, abandoned by God and man, she chooses death so as to remain faithful to her spiritual insights — is felt by a critic like Raknem (*4*, p.254) to be so serious a flaw in the play that he cannot go beyond it to envisage the ironic possibilities implicit in it. I would argue, however, that the coronation scene is the last stroke in an almost Brechtian process of 'alienation' which, quite deliberately, frees us from identifying ourselves emotionally with Joan's long ordeal and agony at the stake in order to permit us to judge with detachment the truth or otherwise of the official legend of her life. Our feelings are checked and cooled by our being forced to move so abruptly from Joan's last breath — 'O Rouen, Rouen, tu seras donc ma dernière demeure? ... O Jésus!' (p.135) — and the murmured prayers for the dead, to Beaudricourt's bustling entry, the scurry of activity among the actors as the funeral pyre is dismantled, the rapid erection of the altar, and the great final burst of sound and colour. However, before this last, visually powerful effect breaks on us, two voices are heard which try and preempt the meaning that we are to derive from the image of the coronation. The first is Charles's: 'La vraie fin de l'histoire de Jeanne est joyeuse. Jeanne d'Arc, c'est une histoire qui finit bien!' (p.137). The second is that of Joan's father upbraiding her brother: 'Prends modèle sur ta sœur! Regarde comme elle est à l'honneur, qu'on se sent fier d'être son père! ... J'avais toujours

dit, moi, que cette petite avait de l'avenir...' (p.137). Both are
commending the official legend of Joan's life as epitomized by
the coronation at Rheims. But, given the structure of feeling
available to us in the rest of the play, and the conventional
nature of its characterization, we are surely not disposed to trust
the judgement of either Charles or the father. The whole thrust
of the play has been so designed as to show Charles up as a
pathetic figure of fun, when he is not otherwise presented as
contemptible in his opportunism and ingratitude. In a
comparable way, Joan's father is projected as a rustic buffoon
and a bully. In a word, Anouilh has placed these conventional
judgements of Joan's life in the mouths of a royal booby and a
self-interested oaf precisely in order that we as spectators should
reject them. In this way we are alerted to the essential falsity of
what is to follow.

Pictorially Anouilh's '... belle image de livre de prix' quite
overshadows anything in Shaw's *Saint Joan*. Indeed, as Shaw's
celebrated preface to the play makes clear, he resisted well-
meaning advice to inflate the spectacular elements and produce a
play in which the coronation 'would eclipse all previous
theatrical displays...' (5, p.65). Instead, he invented the
'Epilogue', a device intended to show up the 'attempts of
posterity to make amends for that execution' (5, p.58). One of
the objects of the Epilogue, in which Charles VII encounters
Ladvenu and the ghosts of Joan and the principal figures at her
trial, was to show that, as no one spoke in Joan's favour during
her trial, none dared speak against her during the rehabilitation.
In fact, the Epilogue is an exercise in comic deflation, intended
to destroy retrospectively the apparently invincible power of
orthodoxy, to show that saints (like geniuses) have the last
laugh, and to mock political and ecclesiastical trimmers and
opportunists. In the changed perspective created by the
Epilogue, Joan's life is revealed as a triumph.

Here, it appears to me, Anouilh has exploited the art of
dramatic echo or quotation so pervasive in his theatre. He has
borrowed from Shaw's Epilogue the notion of ending
L'Alouette with a dramatic device which subverts the
conventional legend that forms the subject of his play. But,

unlike Shaw, he has actually risked exploiting the spectacle of the coronation as his chosen vehicle for conveying the irony which is provided in *Saint Joan* by the Epilogue. Again, unlike Shaw, Anouilh has done so in order to discredit the received idea that the true meaning of Joan's life is to be discovered in her consecrated status as the supreme symbol of French nationalism and patriotism. One is encouraged by the very tawdriness of the coronation scene to recognize that Anouilh's bold and open exploitation of stage illusion is intended to expose the hollowness of official legend. Indeed, the immediate impression made on us by the coronation scene is that it is blatantly *specious*, precisely the sort of transformation scene one might expect in certain kinds of popular theatre, but quite disconnected from the scene of the burning which precedes it. With its pealing organs, chiming bells, salvoes of artillery, illuminated windows, and ceremonial release of doves, this coronation provides a garish excess of stage effects, verging on parody of the stage director's art and of the boulevard public's notorious love of happy endings. It is so contrived as to elicit a shoddy emotional response from the theatre audience and to project an illusion which is calculated to last only for as long as the curtain is up. Once the curtain falls on 'cette belle image de livre de prix', once the spectacle vanishes, the playgoer himself is led to recognize the spuriousness of what he has seen and of his surrender to mere theatrical sleight of hand.

This coronation, then, is no naive celebration of the Maid of Orleans, but a vehicle for implicating the theatre public in the venality, opportunism, fickleness, and incomprehension of true moral grandeur that are manifested by the on-stage representatives of the French nation and, we may infer, of humanity at large. Insofar as the spectators, like the stage characters, assent to this fairy tale in which all comes right in the end, they too are condemned for their shallowness. They are, if only temporarily, taken in by the ritual pomp of that final dazzling scene, failing to grasp that it is empty, unconnected with, and external to, the truth of Joan's life. This is what Grossvogel argues in a clumsy but insightful passage: 'The spectator's customary vision of Jeanne... allows him to

appropriate an ending that pertains to the world disavowed by
Jeanne and thus projects the spectator into the play, making him
and his vision part of, and participant in, the domain rejected'
(*15*, p.195). In this sense, *L'Alouette* offers a distinctive moral
perspective of its own.

That perspective confirms the dramatist's profound
pessimism about the fate of brave idealists in the sordid world of
compromise and self-interest. The effect of all this theatrical
manipulation has been to persuade us that the authorized
version of Joan's life, exemplified by the political and patriotic
'triumph' of the coronation of Charles VII at Rheims, violates
the true significance of her experience. For Anouilh, that truth is
located in her complete moral integrity, in the heroic courage
with which she ultimately refuses to betray those personal
insights which compose her innermost self and make her truly
Joan of Arc. Church and state attempt to wrest from her the
significance which she wants to accord to her experiences and to
take them over for their own purposes. Her glory, for Anouilh,
lies in not submitting to them. The fact that Joan believed
herself to be in direct contact with the saints matters little to
Anouilh; what matters is her refusal to deny her promptings of
conscience under political and ecclesiastical duress. But to say
that is not necessarily to say that Anouilh has actually
discovered a theatrical form worthy of the intense and
exemplary passion he has chosen to deal with. Certainly he has
invented a superb ironic engine, admirably adapted to the
function of destroying the complacent official legend and
exposing the self-deceiving nature of the public mind, but his
technical command and adroitness, his relentless spirit of play,
tend in the long run to distract us from Joan's inwardness and
spiritual ordeal, to frame her in too many vigorous and
colourful scenes that vulgarize and coarsen her rather than
render her as simple, natural, and touching in her naive belief.
Ultimately, *L'Alouette* works at the level of a spirited and ironic
contrivance that confirms our distrust of institutions and feeds
our cynicism about human motives. Yet Joan is not only about
being true to oneself; she is also about a certain heroic aspiration
to serve God. I am not at all sure that the armoury of theatrical

tricks deployed by Anouilh is suited to render that.

(iii)

Pauvre Bitos might be said to have been written under the sign of two of Anouilh's maxims which, in equating life with the life of the stage, typify his confusion of the ethical and the aesthetic. The first occurs in Act I of *La Répétition*, originally performed in October 1950: 'Il fallait aller au défunt Odéon pour trouver plus cabot qu'un procureur de la Haute Cour, réclamant la mort de quelqu'un' (*PB*, p.357) — a sentence which seems positively to look forward to Bitos. The second figures in 'Février 1945', Anouilh's recollections of Brasillach's trial and execution, which first appeared in the extreme right-wing magazine, *Défense de l'Occident*, in February 1955: 'L'histoire n'est pas fameuse. Ces gros effets de théâtre, ce mélo absurde, ces pitreries sinistres, ces traîtres à demi ridicules et puant la convention, avec leurs uniformes, leurs Légions d'honneur, leur gloire, leurs grands mots — c'était bien elle, c'était la vie' (*7*, p.180).

In *L'Alouette* the juggling with time and the insertion of plays within a play offer themselves as eminently theatricalist devices, skilfully chosen so as to make us aware that we are witnessing the ritual reenactment of a fabled life. Insofar as we are drawn into the recurring convention of stage performance and respond to it, it is because we increasingly feel it to be an ambitious and thought-out device consistent with the moral perspective which gradually emerges from the play. In *Pauvre Bitos* everything starts more blatantly from that primary kind of dramatic performance which arises when friends dress up and improvise parts for their own amusement. When Anouilh adopts this model of the *charade* as the central dramatic device of his play, he already seems to me to create a form that provides for an almost flippant degree of detachment from the experiences to be enacted. Not that flippancy need imply geniality. It can be, and in *Pauvre Bitos* emphatically is, caustic to the point of ferocity. And this initial sense of improvisation, of simple play-acting, which we experience as the characters come on stage at the beginning of Act I, is subsequently reinforced by the frequent and knowing allusions to classic texts of Molière, by the constant recourse to the vocabulary of stage performance, and by the insistent way in which acting is presented as mere histrionics. Thus, while *L'Alouette* and *Pauvre Bitos* both exploit the metaphor of the stage in projecting the lives of their characters, *Pauvre Bitos* so handles the metaphor as to intensify the sense of artifice, even meretriciousness, attaching to the performance.

It is in the nature of charades that the disguise should be transparent, and the convention of the 'dîner de têtes', in which historical personages are merely hinted at through the use of an appropriate wig (with, perhaps, the addition of a small item of dress or minimal makeup) is perfectly attuned to the needs of a charade. In *Pauvre Bitos* there can be no question of our entertaining the illusion that the twentieth-century characters are anything other than themselves. Whereas the inner plays of *L'Alouette* cohere with the imagined world of the outer play, in *Pauvre Bitos* we are never allowed to escape the incongruity that comes from seeing a mid-twentieth-century suit or dress topped by an eighteenth-century *perruque*. Such a device totally checks any illusion we might harbour about being 'in history'; the incongruity guarantees an even more pronounced detachment from the action, and an even more acute sense of playful complicity with the dramatist, than any we experience in *L'Alouette*. When Maxime congratulates Deschamps on so quickly grasping the point of the role (Camille Desmoulins) he is to play, he says (p.42): 'Sous le masque de Camille... Je vois que nous nous sommes compris'. But here the language is figurative: the 'mask' is simply Deschamps's assumed part, not an effective disguise. It is a way of connecting a heavily stylized eighteenth century with a twentieth century almost as strongly stylized in the dichotomy it offers between provincial aristocrats and the 'common people'.

The structure of *Pauvre Bitos* is simpler than that of *L'Alouette*. The inter-traffic between past and present in Act I is accomplished at the level of a dinner-table debate in which the guests merely undertake to represent the views of the historical figures they are meant to portray, though with a growing

intensity of personal involvement as the act proceeds.
takes the form of a flashback in which the dream
unconscious Bitos projects us into the period of the F.
Revolution and allows the guests at Maxime's dinner party t
to impersonate leading politicians of the Terror while still
wearing the clothes appropriate to post-Liberation French
society. Act III returns us to the present, but the debate about
ends and means, idealism and fanaticism that has dominated
Act II now peters out in a few cynical incidentals about the
exercise of power and is no longer connected with acts of
impersonation. In such a structure, the constant and rapid
temporal shifts which characterize *L'Alouette* are replaced by a
single major dislocation of the time-scheme that, inventively and
with marked dramatic energy, creates a symbolic dimension in
which the moral conflicts implicit in Act I are intensified and
transformed from the private to the public, the particular to the
general.

I do not think we can pass from this dimension to the
pettiness, uncertain tone and sour farce of Act III without recognizing that the insights and revelations of Act II have not been
used by Anouilh so as to transform the personal relationships
between the characters in Act III. These remain untouched,
static; and a critic like Howarth plausibly argues, in the preface
to his edition of the play (p.24), that this might be accounted a
failure on Anouilh's part to connect Acts II and III in an organic
and satisfying way. There is such a failure, but I do not think it
hinges on the absence of any development of character since
Anouilh is simply interested in showing characters to be moral
essences or types, unchanging and unchangeable, and only
capable of becoming more truly their given selves. The failure
springs essentially from Anouilh's inability to maintain Act III
at the same deeply felt level of argument he provides in Act II. In
this sense, the historical dream-sequence, the grand charade of
Act II, is nothing more than a device for allowing the characters
of Act I to act out their natures more completely and to embody
conflicting ideas. In fact, not only is the insistence on
impersonation, on the acting out of given parts, even more
strikingly present here than in *L'Alouette*, but the purely

conventional nature of impersonation is pushed to its limit
through the use which Anouilh makes of the charade in *Pauvre
Bitos*.

We are psychologically prepared for Bitos, long before he
comes on stage, by the exchanges between Maxime and his
guests which occupy the first fifteen pages of Act I, but when his
entry comes (p.46), it is carefully managed so as to produce the
maximum theatrical effect. The stage directions are explicit:
'*Bitos paraît en haut des marches, il est en Robespierre de la tête
aux pieds sous un manteau noir étriqué et son melon. Quand
Charles le lui prend, il apparaît en bleu ciel*'. It is from this
moment, as Maxime significantly observes (p.47), that the 'game
begins', and this single graphic image instantly establishes Bitos
as an incongruous figure of fun, physically clumsy and socially
inept. His bowler hat literally crowns his incongruity and, in a
striking confirmation of Anouilh's determination to underline
the charade-like character of the play, it is self-consciously
placed on Bitos's head at two particularly significant moments
in the inner play of Act II. The first such moment follows on the
flashback to Robespierre's school days and immediately
precedes that in which the timid young deputy's interview with
Mirabeau epitomizes the gulf between the aristocratic
paternalism of the one and the radical populism of the other.
The actual scene in which the schoolboy Robespierre is chastised
for his pride (pp.78-80) already conveys the strong impression of
a charade since the adult Bitos/Robespierre functions in it as a
kind of chorus, supplying the answers which the mute child-
actor, who is playing Robespierre as a boy, is supposed to return
to the Jesuit schoolmaster. The shift from this moment to the
interview with Mirabeau is then signalled to us in the stage
directions, which specify: '*Il va chercher le chapeau melon de
Bitos et son petit pardessus noir qui étaient dans un coin. Il les
met et va s'asseoir timidement, sur le bord des fesses, sur une
chaise*' (p.80). So we move naturally, and with great dramatic
economy, from one encounter with archaic authority to another
(from Church to feudal nobility) and are led, through the self-
consciously playful use of the bowler hat to connect Robespierre
as a boy, Robespierre as a man, and Bitos, the twentieth-century

inheritor of the revolutionary tradition. At the same time, we recognize the powerful element of make-believe which is operating here, an element which inhibits any impulse we might feel to enter sympathetically into the character's predicament. The bowler hat figures equally deftly in another scene, and creates a similar effect. This occurs at the end of the long monologue (pp.99-100) given to Robespierre after Tallien's dinner party breaks up and the rival politicians of the Terror have gone home. Robespierre is left alone centre-stage and, glowering malevolently at the audience like the stock stage villain, uncovers for our benefit the roots of his puritanical fanaticism in a menacing outburst directed against women: 'Je vous apprendrai, moi! Je vous ferai veuves' (p.100). Precisely at this point, he puts on Bitos's coat and bowler, so merging in a single vivid image the architect of the Terror and the vengeful public prosecutor of the twentieth century. In doing so, he briefly annuls time and space and recalls us to the *performance* which we are witnessing.

Certainly this idea of a charade is what reminds us most insistently of the make-believe nature of what we are seeing, and keeps us at a critical distance from it. As a result of the way in which it works, we are never lost in the experience of the characters but remain constantly alert to the notions of analogy and topicality implicit in the play. However, if the device of the charade works as effectively as it does, it is because it is surrounded by a variety of other theatricalist devices which conduce to the same end. For example, not only is Maxime described as having 'un sens du théâtre étonnant' (p.36), but he acts constantly like a stage director: rehearsing Amanda for her small part (p.37); arranging for Franz/Merda to be 'le Deus ex machina sans lequel nous ne pourrions pas mener à bien la pièce...' (p.43); calling the 'actors' together for the first act — 'Mes enfants, en scène pour le un' (p.46); intervening to retard the forward momentum of the action when the exchanges between the characters in Act I become envenomed — 'Nous allons beaucoup trop vite. Si nous suivons ce train, nous en serons au dix-huit brumaire avant le café...' (p.55). Elsewhere, allusions multiply so as to reinforce this primacy of the

theatrical. The reference to 'l'entrée de l'Exempt' in the last act
of Molière's *Tartuffe* — 'C'est drôle, c'est toujours à cette scène
que moi je perds tout plaisir au Tartuffe...' (p.44), and the
comparison in Act III (p.111) between the fatuous vanity of
Bitos and that of the valet Mascarille in *Les Précieuses ridicules*,
both underline the persistent tendency to see all life in the light
of the stage, especially the comic stage. There is even a moment
in Act III when Brassac is presented like a figure from a Punch
and Judy show — 'Il a disparu à nouveau comme un diable dans
une boîte' (p.107). Nor does the process stop there. Episodes in
history must also be reduced to a sort of dramatic performance,
a glittering first night, in which Danton has the starring role as a
'character-part', Camille Desmoulins plays the 'juvenile lead',
and even the outcome of Danton's trial is seen in terms of
'plotting' and suspense: 'Le problème passionnant pour les
initiés était de savoir comment on empêcherait Danton de
parler...' (p.54). In the same way, Mirabeau's advice to the
aspiring Robespierre is couched in language which suggests that
politics is pure theatre and that public figures, like opera singers,
should be keenly aware of the effects they produce: 'nous
sommes au théâtre... Il faut donc apprendre le métier de
tragédien...' (p.82). Ironically, though Robespierre furiously
rebuffs Mirabeau's cynical condescension, his own favoured
Festival of the Supreme Being actually converts politics into a
kind of street theatre, complete with processions, dancing and
singing (p.103).

Elsewhere again, a vein of mocking self-consciousness alerts
us to the unreal or acted up character of certain moments in the
play. One thinks of Bitos's reply to Vulturne's enquiry after his
mother's welfare: 'Merci, Monsieur le comte, comme on dit
dans les mauvais mélodrames...' (p.63), the uneasy tone of
which suggests not only Bitos's suspicion and lack of social poise
but the way in which the dramatist tends to present all human
relations in terms of the performing of roles. Indeed, when
Deschamps recalls (p.64) the episode in which Bitos's mother
pleads with him for the life of the young *milicien* Lucien and
slaps him hard across the face when he declines to intervene, the
incident is so rendered, in tone and language, that it appears to

belong to the convention of traditional melodrama rather than to the harsh realities of common life.[6] There seems to be no escape in this play from a kind of self-advertising artifice, and this is compounded by the manifestly implausible plotting. Not only has Franz Delanoue conveniently been released from prison just in time to assist in Maxime's squalid little scheme, but Bitos has, that very afternoon, been rejected as Victoire's suitor. Added to this is the distinct improbability that an old *maquis* fighter like Deschamps would be ready to join forces with a bunch of vicious and idle aristocrats in order to humiliate a former comrade like Bitos, no matter how much he may now disapprove of him.

Then there is the matter of Anouilh's recourse to farce. In the inevitable anticlimax which follows on 'Merda's' shooting of Bitos/Robespierre, the action of Act III flags and threatens to fall into an embarrassed naturalism. We feel the banality of it all as Bitos dries himself before leaving and his class enemies cast round for a way of detaining him. It is precisely at this moment that Anouilh exercises his ingenuity so as to rescue the idea of a theatrical game. He does this quite simply by opening out the elements of farce. Some period 'heads' are discarded, only to be replaced by something even more fanciful and risible. Brassac takes off his wig but wears instead '*un curieux couvre-pied sur les épaules*' (p.107), and Bitos, soaked through by the thunderstorm, presents a still more ridiculous figure: '*une serviette autour du cou et une sorte de rideau ridicule sur le dos qui lui donne un vague air d'empereur romain*' (p.108). From this moment on, the farcical rhythms of the action accelerate. Bitos is grossly flattered, plied with drink, congratulated on being a lady-killer and a man of the world. Like the provincial booby he remains under the veneer of public authority, he is taken in by it all. The scenes of his increasing drunkenness and folly are pushed to the edge of pantomime because Anouilh frames them in a farcical choreography, with the rest of the cast lavishing compliments and whisky on him as they circle maliciously

[6] My point here is not really affected if one accepts the suggestion made by Comminges (*12*, p.71) that the scene is lifted from Anatole France's novel *Les Dieux ont soif*. In either case, it is a matter of Anouilh preferring art to life.

around. The women 'flutter' about him (p.111); Julien, Brassac and Maxime '*l'entourent, lui tapent sur les épaules...*' (p.113); and when Bitos finally agrees not to take action against Franz Delanoue, his decision is crowned by another piece of farcical stage 'business': '*Les trois hommes se précipitent à la fois avec trois bouteilles*' (p.119). This balletic style of movement is echoed a little later by the flurried movements of the servants as they fetch coats for the departing guests (p.126), just as the initial burlesque image of Bitos, draped in his 'imperial' curtain, is echoed near the climax of these incidents when he is projected as a merciful Augustus, 'de plus en plus César romain...' (p.118). The farcical climax itself is reserved for that moment when Victoire accidentally stumbles on Bitos in the incongruous posture of sticking out his backside so that Charles can mend the tear in the seat of his breeches (p.128). The picture he presents to us destroys the remnants of his dignity and reduces him to the level of a clown.

In Act II the conflicts we witness between the revolutionary 'virtue' of Robespierre and Saint-Just, on the one hand, and the voices of moderation or opportunism (Mirabeau, Danton, Camille Desmoulins, Tallien), on the other, are genuine conflicts of principle, even when mixed with gross personal and selfish motives. Such conflicts engender a moral debate and use a moral language that raise this act above the odious personal vendetta conducted by the petty and vindictive provincial notables whom we encounter in Act I. The sense of local and personal grievance, which is so potent in Act I and pursued with such truculent comic verve, is much attenuated in the almost Shavian debates of Act II, only to surface again in the scenes of sour farce, bordering on slapstick, which we get in Act III. This collapse into farce, achieved by the theatricalist devices I have examined, is a major flaw in the play. It suggests that, in spite of the simplicity of the three-act structure, Anouilh fails to unify the action of the play precisely because he fails to meet the moral and intellectual expectations he himself raises in the debates of Act II. We are invited to repudiate the revolutionary ideology of Bitos and of Robespierre (as if it were the same), but the twentieth-century exponents of moderation, like some of their eighteenth-century precursors, hardly constitute a convincing moral alternative to their enemies. So farce emerges as the dramatic form best suited to articulate a moral impasse. At the end of *Pauvre Bitos* we are left without a shred of optimism; there is no confidence that Frenchmen will ever be capable of transcending the divisions that lacerate their society. In this sense, the farce of Act III reflects the wreck of hope.

contradictions precariously fused. In *L'Alouette* and the
moral dramas with a thesis, however, so, have changes at the
drama, have been more schematic, on a moral narrative. At the
end of *Pauvre Bitos* we are left with a sense of vindicated
virtue, and even that ambiguity until into by Anouilh.

3. *Moral Vision and Stage Types*

(i)

Deft and assured handling of time-shifts and plays within plays,
constant resort to the imagery of stage performance (role-
playing, cues, echoes of theatrical classics), combine, in
L'Alouette and *Pauvre Bitos*, to maintain us in a state of alert
detachment and to persuade us of the essentially artificial and
illusory nature of what we are seeing. Both *L'Alouette* and
Pauvre Bitos form part of that remarkably consistent imaginary
universe created by Anouilh in successive plays since the nineteen thirties. If one excepts the impassioned naturalism of
certain early plays like *L'Hermine* (1932), *Jézabel* (written 1932)
and *La Sauvage* (1938, but written 1934), and even these borrow
much from the heavy stylization of melodrama, this consistency
comes first from Anouilh's adoption of a resilient, inventive,
but fundamentally unchanging, theatricalist technique of the
kind delineated above. Secondly, it derives from the constancy
and simplicity of his moral vision; too simple to command a full
intellectual assent once it is divorced from its theatrical context,
but plausible and even seductive when articulated through
Anouilh's chosen conventions and characters.

The moral vision embodied in these early dramas of Anouilh,
in which the tone and substance are intensely serious and only
very partially and ambiguously distanced by theatricalist devices
(use of stock characters, knowing exploitation of the
conventions of melodrama), is structured about a series of
extreme antitheses in which purity is set against corruption,
revolt against resignation, and no-saying against yea-saying. In
such plays, the world is envisaged as a place of failure, moral
degradation and despair, and there tends to be a single dominant
'voice' (easily identifiable with the author) on whom all
attention is lavished and who, as Harvey perceptively notes (*17*,

p.37), is usually surrounded by caricatures or 'lifeless agents' created merely to elicit responses from the 'hero'. These heroes are isolated and exceptional figures and constitute a true 'band of the Elect', as it has been said. They are engaged in an urgent struggle to attain not some form of commonplace happiness, which in fact they despise, but a pure and perfect love, a kind of self-transcendence which is quite unrealizable in the shifting and mundane world of habit, inertia, compromise and corruption in which they are compelled to live. They are not, in any formal sense, religious but the intensity of their idealism is such that, as their language frequently discloses, they are prone to confusing sacred and profane, harbour impossible expectations and, in the last resort, are doomed to failure.

I believe that in Anouilh's early dramas he quite consciously borrows from the conventions of melodrama but that the model he has chosen slips out of his control, so that there are scenes in which he is not so much exploiting melodrama as overwhelmed by it. However, such a dramatic form does, at least, allow the moral logic implicit in the characters' ideals to find its natural (which is to say, pessimistic) end through a plot which emphasizes the imperviousness of a compromised and compromising society to the moral energies of lonely idealists. The *pièces roses* of the same period — *Le Bal des voleurs* (1938), *Léocadia* (1940), *Le Rendez-vous de Senlis* (1941) — deflect this logic through the exercise of make-believe. In these escapist plays fancy reigns supreme. The constraints of mundane reality are removed: pain, frustration, disillusionment are short-circuited as disguise, impersonation, the spirit of play, all combine to invent happy solutions. The plays Anouilh wrote from 1941 onwards depart significantly from those composed before the war. The genial comedies of fancy, full of poetic charm and buoyancy, disappear, as though they had represented a privileged, but transient, moment in which Anouilh's native pessimism was permitted to fall into abeyance. At the same time, the theatricalist devices and imagery which had characterized them become more elaborate and are generalized over the whole range of his production. The lines between 'drama' and 'comedy' get blurred, elements of comedy or farce infiltrating 'serious' treatments of myth and legend, and elements of near-tragic intensity penetrating comedy and farce. These technical developments seem to me to represent the formal equivalent in Anouilh's theatre of a deeply pessimistic vision of life in which no valid and satisfying moral order exists capable of giving meaning to man's experience. The human craving for moral absolutes (utter purity or total integrity) and the sense of disillusionment which comes from realizing that such absolutes are, at best, unattainable in the sordid world of everyday trans-actions and, at worst, self-destructive, generates in the early dramas a despair which is temporarily eclipsed in the total artifice of the *pièces roses* and then surfaces again to inform Anouilh's later plays, including *L'Alouette* and *Pauvre Bitos*.

I think Anouilh's increasing theatricalism is very significant. The higher the incidence of images and effects tending to suggest that 'All the world's a stage ...', and consequently, the greater the density of *illusion* available to us in Anouilh's plays, the greater seems to be the intensity of moral disillusion they express. A critic like Borgal (*11*, p.102) actually argues that Anouilh's self-conscious play with theatricalist language and conventions represents a kind of 'aestheticism', a way of evading the despair that comes from acknowledging that the world is unlivable for uncompromising idealists in search of moral absolutes. This may well be true of the *pièces roses*, but elsewhere Anouilh's theatricalism becomes a way of *registering* moral impasse rather than avoiding it. The concentration of images and vocabulary drawn from the life of the stage actually expresses, and sometimes in a very showy fashion, an authentic sense of despair, a profound feeling for the emptiness of human life. It is true that the moral absolutism which is clearly intended to elicit our sympathy, and sometimes our admiration, for the rebels of the early dramas (especially Thérèse of *La Sauvage*), continues to exercise a powerful appeal when embodied in figures of ancient myth like Orphée and Antigone, or legendary national characters like Joan of Arc and Becket, even when we are uncertain about some of the values that move them. However, such intransigent idealism is altogether less persuasive in the romantic death-wish of *Roméo et Jeannette* (1946), and is plainly offered for our condemnation in the self-destructive frenzy of *Médée* (1953) and the inhuman fanaticism of *Pauvre Bitos*. Indeed, the moral extremism which had the force of an ethical imperative in Anouilh's early theatre, is shown in most of the post-war plays to be a kind of dangerous madness and an enemy of life. Our dramatist either makes a laughing-stock of it in his farces or raises it to the level of a horror cartoon in emblematic figures like Médée, the Inquisitor of *L'Alouette* and Robespierre in *Pauvre Bitos*.

It has to be stressed that this evolving moral sense in Anouilh's theatre is inseparable from the theatricalist conventions through which it is articulated. Hence 'character' is an extension of the pervasive metaphor of the stage, and there are moments in Anouilh's plays when such a view of characterization is given explicit expression. Cauchon's insistence in *L'Alouette* that each character has to play out the role allotted to him — 'Nous ne pouvons que jouer nos rôles ...' (p.55) — simply restates what is said in *Antigone*: 'A chacun son rôle. Lui, il doit nous faire mourir, et nous, nous devons aller enterrer notre frère' (*NPN*, p.144). And this formula, with its implication that personages of the drama are always consistent, always behave 'in character', is more elaborately spelt out for us in *Eurydice* when Monsieur Henri defines life in terms of antithetical types: 'Mon cher, il y a deux races d'êtres. Une race nombreuse, féconde, heureuse, une grosse pâte à pétrir, qui mange son saucisson, fait ses enfants, pousse ses outils, compte ses sous, bon an mal an, malgré les épidémies et les guerres, jusqu'à la limite d'âge; des gens pour vivre, des gens pour tous les jours, des gens qu'on n'imagine pas morts. Et puis il y a les autres, les nobles, les héros. Ceux qu'on imagine très bien étendus, pâles, un trou rouge dans la tête, une minute triomphants avec une garde d'honneur ou entre deux gendarmes selon: le gratin' (*PN*, p.440).

The first, we infer, resign themselves, adjust to life, display great powers of survival; the second reject prescribed moral codes, seek an authentic personal morality, and meet a premature end. Such a typology is absurdly novelettish but, modified and inflected, it persists in *L'Alouette* and *Pauvre*

Bitos. It assigns people to excessively narrow and stylized roles
and strictly limits their possibilities. The descriptive detail used
to flesh out this typology, in which life is seen to be divided
between 'peasants' who endure and 'princes' who are doomed to
tragic ends, bears no relationship to modern life and appears to
reflect a sentimental nostalgia for a vanished social and moral
order. There is either gross life, swarming like a Breughel
canvas, or heroic death conveyed by a sensational image
apparently taken from one of the popular Sunday newspapers.
It hardly seems enough to argue here that we are not dealing
with 'real life'. Of course we are not, but the question is whether
these broadly defined types can ever be emblematic of the
variousness and complexity of moral experience, and whether
this does not condemn Anouilh's theatre to a kind of brilliant
superficiality. Certainly, character so conceived does not consist
in the exploration of psychological states or moral attitudes.
Character is flattened to type; it is 'voice' or *persona*, the
convenient embodiment of a fixed nature or moral passion. It is
a necessary consequence of Anouilh's insistence on role and
performance as central elements of human activity that many of
his characters tend to lack human density and particularity, and
to be imprisoned in a kind of fatalism which comes from their
having to act out their unchanging and unchangeable selves.
However, certain of Anouilh's major characters are granted a
due share of singularity. I have in mind the way in which he
lends to even legendary figures like Joan of Arc or Becket a
substantial degree of individuality which removes them from the
flatness of stereotypes though, as Harvey convincingly argues
(*17*, p.44), never to the point of endangering the distance that
the dramatist intends us to keep from his stage characters. This
is not, I think, incompatible with recognizing, as Grossvogel
does (*15*, p.185), that a vivid and highly particularized Eurydice
or Antigone or Médée is difficult to accommodate within the
inherited myth which, in its original form, is greatly concerned
with the values, beliefs and fate of the community as a whole
and much less interested in the private needs and insights of
exceptional individuals.

(ii)

Nothing is more striking in *L'Alouette* and *Pauvre Bitos* than the degree to which characters are reduced to, and echo, a family of types with which Anouilh's earlier plays have made us familiar. The dramatist deploys a technique of self-quotation which reinforces our feeling of entering an autonomous imaginary world. For example, his Joan of Arc sometimes sounds like a reincarnation of earlier rebellious heroines: Thérèse or Antigone or Médée, just as his Inquisitor and Bitos/ Robespierre seem created to embody an inflated and perverted version of the destructive strain present in the idealism of such rebels. Nor is this process of self-quotation confined to the principal antagonists. Joan's family life is painted as less grossly vulgar than that of the heroines of *La Sauvage* and *Eurydice*, but reflects the same shaming qualities of crassness and venality, while Bitos's working-class childhood shares the sordid moral atmosphere of the early dramas and also echoes the paternal brutality of *L'Alouette*. All these families are, in fact, a single highly stylized family. In all this, there is little sense of character as being a response to lived experience, but a strong sense of character as a theatrical counter drawn from a restricted range of types and intended to illustrate the playwright's fixed and schematic moral vision. Indeed, the characters in these plays depict very well the moral evolution within Anouilh's plays which I have traced elsewhere. Consequently, it is good for Joan of Arc to say no because the true voice of conscience is sacred and affirms life, but bad for the sense of this no-saying to be subsequently perverted by church and state and turned into a triumphal myth which serves their own ends. In a comparable way, it is bad for the Inquisitor and for Bitos/Robespierre to say no because their conception of virtue is so fanatically extreme as to deny life. In Anouilh's earliest dramas the anguished rebels are infinitely more appealing and interesting than the lay figures who surround them, and this is equally true of a number of his later plays, but a strenuous effort is made in both *L'Alouette* and *Pauvre Bitos* to ensure that the central protagonists do not overwhelm the others. So Joan of Arc is offset by Cauchon and the Inquisitor, who sometimes rival her in dramatic interest and moral stature, while the weight of Bitos's presence is certainly balanced by that of powerful agents like Maxime, Vulturne and Brassac.

It will be worth looking in greater detail at how Anouilh's technique of characterization is worked out in *L'Alouette*. Joan's own character is, of course, of central importance here. Shaw is more inclined than Anouilh to stress Joan's physical robustness, her general capabilities and her grasp of public affairs. She is a 'born boss', more presumptious and more bumptious than Anouilh's Joan but, though direct and earthy, quite free of the coarseness displayed by Anouilh's warrior-maid. In this respect, Shaw is surely closer to the authentic Joan (always supposing she is actually recoverable by historians) than Anouilh who, in depicting Joan at Court as 'toute seule, toute petite, toute grise ...' (p.84) relegates her to the gallery of his earlier frail heroines of humble origins — Eurydice or Jeannette, for example. However, both Shaw and Anouilh are at one in stressing Joan's peasant good sense, and this quality survives in some of the pert replies which Anouilh borrows from the trial record and revives in the text of *L'Alouette*. Here one senses that what principally appeals to Anouilh, as, coincidentally, it appealed to the eternal *lycéen* in Brasillach, is the rather breath-taking lack of respect for the gravity and authority of the adult world which is betrayed by Joan's pertness. In his rewriting of the proceedings of the trial, Brasillach openly exults in this (*1*, p.19), seeing in Joan an 'image de la vertu d'Insolence' and applauding the way in which she protests '... avec une opiniâtreté presque rieuse, une insolence de fille de la campagne qui se moque des messieurs de la ville...'. On the other hand, her bluff admonition to Warwick, whose fastidiousness will keep him away from the burning, unacceptably reduces our belief in her because it so signally reduces her vulnerability: 'Il faudra avoir du courage, petit gars...' (p.132). This is quite at variance with the terror-stricken reply that the historical record reveals her as having given to Martin Ladvenu and Jean Toutmouillé: 'Ha! Ha! J'aimerais mieux être décapitée sept fois que d'être ainsi brûlée' (*1*, p.147).

For Shaw, Joan is more or less sexless. For Vermorel, she goes to her death both because she wants to stay faithful to the mission she has received from the saints and also because she has lost her virginity to the guards and cannot face her companions in arms any more: 'Moi, soldat, plus jamais je ne pourrais voir des soldats, penser à des soldats, rire avec des soldats, me dévouer à des soldats. Oh, il va falloir toutes ces flammes pour me laver' (*8*, Act IV, Tab.1, p.132). Anouilh replaces this image of Joan witth a curiously ambiguous one. He implies that she successfully fends off the guards and remains a virgin, but he also represents her as possessing a kind of vulgar knowingness in her relations with soldiers. She deflects Beaudricourt's perfunctory lust with an assurance that seems ill-suited to a carefully guarded farmer's daughter: '... Tu en retrouveras d'autres, va, des filles, vilain pourceau, si tu tiens absolument à pécher... Des filles qui te feront plus plaisir et qui te demanderont moins de choses... Moi je ne te plais pas tellement' (p.65). And her candid delight in La Hire's animal appetites, however refreshing a change from the puritanism and suppressed lust of the Promoter, sometimes verges on a sort of louche complicity that is difficult to reconcile with the simple and astonished instrument of heavenly voices: 'Mon gros ours, tu tues, tu jures, tu ne pense qu'aux filles' (p.110). There is an incoherence here that is not convincingly explained away by references to the innocence of what is natural: 'Il est bon comme chacun de mes soldats qui tue, qui viole, qui pille, qui jure... Il est bon comme vos loups, mon Dieu, que vous avez fait innocents...' (p.112). To describe mercenary soldiers as being as 'innocent' as wolves is suspect both as logic and theology, but the speech is there to establish the breadth of Joan's human sympathy and not the impeccable status of her religious beliefs. In accepting and rejoicing in La Hire's animal nature, Joan also accepts that joy and pleasure are part of God's design, but the carnal emphasis is so strong that it tends to relegate the idea of spiritual aspiration to the margins. Certainly, Joan's frank approval of La Hire ('Tu sens bon, La Hire, tu sens la bête, tu sens l'homme') contrasts with the attitudes of earlier Anouilh heroines (Thérèse, Antigone, Jeannette) whose ethical intransigence is often linked with a certain delicacy, even fastidiousness, about the physical expression of love. Indeed, in a number of the earlier plays, from *La Sauvage* to *Roméo et Jeannette*, there is an idealized, and some would say sentimentalized, vocabulary of camaraderie in which the relationships of lovers are desexualized. These early allusions to 'le petit soldat', 'le petit compagnon', 'deux petits frères', are revived in *L'Alouette* (p.111) when Joan speaks of 'botte à botte avec un copain' or 'la vraie chaleur du copain contre leur cuisse...', just as Joan's glee and love of a fight (p.60) recall the quarrelsome children of *Ardèle* (1948) and *Le Boulanger, la boulangère et le petit mitron*.

While Joan's mystical experiences are beyond the range of Shaw's sceptical temper, he goes further than Anouilh in at least contriving some sense of the miraculous in *Saint Joan* — I think particularly of the scene (*5*, Sc. 3) where a sudden wind springs up on Joan's arrival at Orléans. This dimension of miracle-working is resolutely avoided by Anouilh. On the other hand, when Anouilh shows Saint Michael speaking through Joan's mouth, he is assenting, at least in dramatic terms, to the idea of her being possessed by supernatural powers. Shaw's scepticism is generally more open, and more polemically expressed, than anything we encounter in Anouilh, where scepticism is applied to institutional dogma and to legend but not to Joan's own convictions nor to the reality that God has for her.

God is a reality for the Joan of *L'Alouette* as never for the archbishop in Anouilh's *Becket*, whose religion is largely formal and certainly inseparable from the institutional claims of the Church whose rituals he serves. He acts as if God exists but has nothing of Joan's simple trust in her 'voices'. She remains the child of rusticity, he is never less than the high-born aesthete. In what must, I suppose, be accounted an implicit parallel with Christ's passion, the Joan of *L'Alouette* is finally abandoned by all, even by La Hire. This sets her apart from everyone else in the play. For Joan, God is good sense, decency, even thrift (p.100). He works through human will, courage and intelligence in order to perform his miracles (p.101); in this sense, God needs men as men need God. What is more, man must continue to act when God appears to have fallen silent; in Pronko's phrase (*26*, p.71), he must act alone in the midst of a design he cannot be sure of and can never fully comprehend. Though man may be flawed and sinful, he remains 'le vrai miracle de Dieu sur cette terre...' (p.101) and has, indeed, been chosen as God's instrument precisely because of his divided nature, his capacity for good and evil: 'Et Dieu l'avait justement créé pour cette contradiction' (p.102). Essentially, then, Joan trusts in human virtues and capacities (courage, endurance), distrusts institutions, including the family, but accepts both Church and Crown, believing that her spiritual revelations serve both.

The historical Joan relapses because Cauchon's refusal to free her from her chains and let her hear Mass and take the sacraments confirms her in her belief that she has been betrayed by a Church which should have made its consolations available to her. In choosing death, Joan rises above it and her tormentors, and such resolution is the privilege of exceptional spirits, their triumph over a tainted world. So in *L'Alouette* Joan's ultimate readiness to go to the stake is inseparably linked with her refusal to dwindle into anything less than the true self she has discovered through her experience of the divine and her ordeal at the trial. Such a choice is at least as convincing as the decision made by Shaw's Saint Joan not to endure perpetual imprisonment because it will exile her for ever from the world of nature. Initially, Joan's faith may be conventional, part of the inherited order of Catholic belief, but it is so inflected in *L'Alouette* as to become part of the vision that marks the rest of Anouilh's theatre. In fact, in taking her decision, Anouilh's Joan joins the company of his other heroines, exemplified most powerfully by Antigone and Médée, who have died precisely in order to be true to themselves, to become, in an almost Platonic way, the ideal of themselves that is already embodied in their legendary status. The 'true' meaning of their lives is disclosed as lying in their already destined mission. Thus, when Joan declaims defiantly in *L'Alouette*: 'Je vous rends Jeanne! Pareille à elle et pour toujours' (p.132), she awakens echoes of the exultant Médée when everything is in ruins about her: 'Je suis Médée, enfin, pour toujours!' (*NPN*, p.402). And this repudiation of the common lot, this aspiration toward self-transcendence, is at one and the same time a rejection of the compromise and corruption of the world. Such a rejection finds expression in Joan's proud claim in L'Alouette: '... mon droit est de continuer à croire et de vous dire non' (p.99). Here L'Alouette is certainly echoing the heroine's reply to Créon in Anouilh's Antigone: 'Je ne veux pas comprendre. C'est bon pour vous. Moi, je suis là pour autre chose que pour comprendre. Je suis là pour vous dire non et pour mourir' (NPN, p.184). This itself may well be an echo of Vermorel's Jeanne avec nous, performed in the same year (1942) as Antigone was being written: '... cette fille qui a surtout su dire "non"...' (8, Act IV, Tab. 2, p.140). In the same way, Joan's wry words in Jeanne avec nous — 'Tu vois une Jeanne vieillie, et qui a réussi, bien installée dans le succès, à qui le goût du marchandage est venu avec l'embonpoint...' (8, Act IV, p.132) — strikingly prefigure those of L'Alouette: 'Vous voyez Jeanne ayant vécu, les choses s'étant arrangées... Jeanne délivrée, peut-être, végétant à la Cour de France d'une petite pension' (p.131). All of which tends to confirm the fact that Joan is only to a limited degree drawn from 'life' (which is to say, from history), but principally taken from Anouilh's own imaginary universe or borrowed from other imagined worlds, notably those created by Shaw and Vermorel.

Other figures in the play also conform to Anouilh's established typology of character. Official religion as epitomized by the Archbishop is characterized by purely conventional faith, worldliness and political sophistication. It can be said of him, in stark contrast to Cauchon or the Inquisitor, that his religious terminology is superficial. Both the Archbishop and Charles expound a view of religion that echoes the near-superstition expressed in Roméo et Jeannette (1946) where Lucien is all for letting sleeping gods lie (NPN, p.279). The Archbishop's own fervent wish never to attract God's attention (p.83) may well echo a moment in a celebrated play of Giraudoux, one of Anouilh's most admired models. It comes in a speech in Electre when Egisthe voices his cardinal principle of statesmanship: '... il est hors de doute que la règle première de tout chef d'état est de veiller férocement à ce que les dieux ne soient point secoués de cette léthargie...'.[7] Charles's view of the deity is not very different: 'C'est l'arbitre et il marque les points. Et, en fin de compte, il est toujours avec ceux qui ont beaucoup d'argent et de grosses armées' (p.90). This piece of royal cynicism is almost certainly borrowed from Shaw's 'God is on the side of the big battalions' (5, Sc. 5, p.135), even if the epigram originally derives from Voltaire. Charles utters this phrase when he is introducing Joan to the game of cards, and so the imagery of card-playing enhances the idea of a detached God presiding over the human game of chance, an idea at variance with Catholic doctrine. Essentially, Charles and the Archbishop distrust the claims of high idealism and are ready to settle for a quiet life. Their willingness to shift, scheme and compromise is exactly what Anouilh sets out to discredit in the abject parents of *La Sauvage* and *Eurydice*, and even perhaps in Créon's weary statesmanship in *Antigone*. But it is this very readiness which, in many post-war plays, is viewed with increasing sympathy and understanding, just as it is the apologists for compromise who come to be seen as preferable to the visionaries whose pursuit of impossible dreams brings the world crashing about our ears.

In *L'Alouette* Joan of Arc eludes this schematic dichotomy between destructive idealists and humane compromisers because her act of self-sacrifice causes no harm to others. In that act, as in her acceptance of man's flawed nature, she reveals that the aspiration toward purity or total integrity is acceptable when rooted in love. As a result, the conflict between fanatical principle and humane compromise has to be transposed into a struggle between certain antithetical types who surround Joan: on the one hand, the Inquisitor and the Promoter who is his parody; on the other, Cauchon, his secular counterpart, Warwick, and the timid Charles. The Inquisitor is truly terrible in his theological rigour. He is the fierce guardian of orthodoxy because he profoundly believes that orthodoxy embodies God's truth and that departure from it obscures truth and opens the floodgates to all forms of extravagance, eccentricity and hysteria. To sin is to place one's own insights above the

---

[7] Jean Giraudoux, *Electre* (Paris, Grasset, 1952), p.42. Originally staged by Louis Jouvet in May 1937.

accumulated institutionalized wisdom of the Church Militant, and the sinner who resists the authority of reigning orthodoxy is a living danger to the existing order: 'Tant qu'il restera un homme qui ne sera pas brisé, l'Idée, même si elle domine et broie tout le reste du monde, sera en danger de périr' (p.115). It follows that the pursuit of dissenters must be implacable, untainted by wishy-washy sentiment, and free of any tendency to confuse the milk of human kindness with the exigent theological virtue of charity. In this light, human frailty cannot be tolerated: it is not a quality but a defect: 'jeunesse, générosité, tendresse humaine sont des noms d'ennemis... Et qui aime l'homme, n'aime pas Dieu' (p.105). It is not simply the intransigence of these principles that chills but the total indifference to fallible mortals which they imply. Anouilh's Inquisitor, awesomely relentless when compared with his historical original, is ready to make a wilderness and call it obedience. The intensity of his theological convictions depersonalizes and dehumanizes him. Set beside the Inquisitor, the Promoter is almost a figure of fun, perhaps designed by Anouilh as a means of reducing the painfully oppressive atmosphere of parts of the trial. He can be dangerous in his lack of restraint and his self-serving determination to be the obedient tool of his ecclesiastical masters, but ultimately he remains a contemptible clerical *apparatchik*, a bureaucrat who quite lacks the intellectual stature, coherence and sense of mission which mark everything the Inquisitor says.

The Inquisitor's iron inflexibility is the enemy of life and the contrary both of the Archbishop's venality and of the simplicity, directness and humanity of Joan's beliefs. In depicting Cauchon sympathetically as a disinterested and merciful agent of the Church, Anouilh discards the Bishop of Beauvais's historically authenticated ambition, opportunism and zeal in prosecuting Joan, and concentrates instead on his humane concern and feeling for men's weakness. In this way, he emerges as a satisfying antithesis to the Inquisitor's inhumanity, and so contributes to the play's dramatic symmetry and balance. There is about Cauchon, in Anouilh's version of the story, a largeness of spirit that is conspicuously absent from the other two examples of moderation (Warwick and Charles) who also serve in the play as a counterpoise to the deadly fanaticism of the Inquisitor. As with the Inquisitor, Cauchon has his shadow in the person of Ladvenu, but this priest is rendered without caricature as a servant of the system who has not forfeited compassion. Cauchon himself is projected as admirably patient, even magnanimous. He ignores the near impertinence of some of Joan's answers — 'Une plaisanterie n'a jamais été une réponse, Jeanne...' (p.98); protects her against the incorrigible zeal of the Promoter, especially on the charges of superstition and sorcery — 'Il nous faut laisser quelques fées aux petites filles, dans notre propre intérêt' (p.45). He pleads for her understanding of the Church's position; warns her gently when pride and impetuousness lead her into making statements that are harmful to her own interest — 'Ne t'enferme pas dans ton orgueil, Jeanne' (p.99); and loses his temper only so as to save her from the brink of perdition: 'Tu dois pourtant comprendre que c'est mon dernier geste pour toi, que je n'en pourrai plus d'autre' (p.120). All this helps to invest Cauchon with a degree of individuality which rescues him from conventional flatness and permits him to emerge as the voice of responsible and humane authority as against the fanaticism of the Inquisitor.

By contrast, Anouilh's Warwick and Charles remain stage types largely derived from the theatre of Bernard Shaw. In important respects, the first is very much Shaw's gentleman at large who symbolizes the self-interest and appetite for power which the English governing classes hide under the cloak of formal good manners. The second recalls the Shavian anti-hero — Shaw's own Dauphin, the Swiss mercenary Bluntschli of *Arms and the Man*, the legendary but deflated Don Juan in Act III of *Man and Superman* — who refuses to live up to the heroic expectations which others entertain of him. Anouilh's Warwick, who was played in the original Paris production with a marked English accent that was, perhaps, intended to appeal to traditional anglophobia, certainly echoes Shaw's satire of the English fondness for self-righteously justifying national and selfish interests. But Anouilh adds to the conventional image a convention of his own that recurs in several of his plays. This is

his tendency to posit grace as a class virtue and to equate the
aristocracy with taste and aesthetic refinement. More than once,
these qualities are symbolized by Warwick's fastidious sniffing
at a rose (p.44, p.56), and by his use of a certain kind of
aesthetic vocabulary which he applies to moral issues. Hence,
unnecessary suffering is dismissed as 'inelegant' (p.129) or
'vulgar' (p.131), just as the mocked-up Coronation scene is
criticized for being in 'bad taste' (p.136).

Warwick lives by the code of a stage English gentleman. His
snobbery is highly conventional too. His contempt for trades-
men of every sort embraces even a great nobleman like the duc
de Bourgogne when the latter exacts his price for acting as an
intermediary between the French and the English (p.42). Here
Anouilh copies Shaw's witty aside in *Saint Joan* (5, p.113), with
its allusion to 'three or four middlemen' expecting their cut
before Joan can be handed over to the English. This echo of
Shaw is complicated and enriched for the Parisian theatre-going
public of 1953 by memories of the hard-faced businessmen who
had done well out of the recent German occupation. Anouilh
also follows Shaw in depicting Warwick as a sceptic and
materialist who dismisses credulous accounts of Joan's armour
and banner, and even her status as a warrior-maid, as so many
'children's tales' (p.40). As with Shaw, Anouilh's Warwick is
very much the subtle politician who aims to discredit Charles's
coronation by discrediting Joan's claims to have received divine
guidance. Raknem (4, p.254) thinks it inconsistent to show
Warwick as wanting Joan's death at the beginning of the play
but as wanting to rescue her from the stake toward the end, but
such a view fails to appreciate the political skills which Anouilh,
in the manner of Shaw, grants to Warwick. In fact, Joan's
recantation will serve admirably both to discredit Charles and to
prevent the Maid from being converted into a popular martyr
(p.126).

As for Charles the Dauphin, he stems at least as much from
Shaw as from national legend, though here again Anouilh
succeeds in reconciling the Shavian elements with his own conventions of characterization. In *L'Alouette* Joan handles him
skilfully, playing on his resentment of the ambitious courtiers

who intimidate him, but she is less bluff and managing than Shaw's Joan. The Dauphin himself is every bit as childish, timid and opportunistic in Anouilh's version as in Shaw's, but sillier in the newly acquired self-importance that makes him insist on being addressed as 'Sire' by Joan, should she ever return to Court (p.128). Anouilh's Charles is also more odious in expressing openly his relief at being freed of any sense of obligation to Joan once she has recanted: '... je n'aime pas qu'on se dévoue pour moi. Je n'aime pas qu'on m'aime. Cela vous crée des obligations. Et j'ai horreur des obligations' (p.127). But it is in his sensual appetites and the abjectness with which he bears with a life full of petty humiliations that Charles aligns himself with those earlier character-types in Anouilh's theatre who exemplify venality, compromise and the flight from challenging and exacting ideals. It is a paradox that, young though he is, he seems to belong naturally to the family of Anouilh's awful middle-aged defeatists.

Apart from Joan herself, the women characters are largely 'flat': her mother an intimidated housewife absorbed in domesticity; Agnes and the Queen empty and frivolous beneficiaries of royal bounty; the Queen Mother, Yolande, a cynical schemer in a man's world. The only other feminine qualities are those embodied in La Hire's whores, who figure in the dialogue but not in the action. In this way, Anouilh's familiar dichotomy between rebel idealists and tainted conformists is sustained throughout *L'Alouette*, and any possibility of individualizing the female characters is sacrificed to that primary effect of moral and dramatic symmetry. This technique of conventional characterization is finally, if marginally, displayed in the common soldier Boudousse who echoes the stupid and time-serving auxiliaries of state power whom we meet among the guards in *Antigone* and again in the prison warders of *Pauvre Bitos*.

(iii)

In spite of many differences of tone, emphasis and detail, *Pauvre Bitos* recognizably continues the highly conventional

characterization that is a feature of *L'Alouette* and draws on
Anouilh's established typology of rebels and conformists,
austere idealists and venal compromisers. It also follows
L'Alouette in depicting the destructive consequences of miscon-
ceived idealism, though it does so by exploiting a style of
invective and a range of topical allusions that greatly enhance
the immediacy and ferocity of its impact. Though the historical
characters of *L'Alouette* are recreated in terms of Anouilh's
already established imaginary universe, they effectively cohere
in important respects with the authentic historical figures whom
they represent. However, in the way in which he exploits the
device of the charade in *Pauvre Bitos*, Anouilh sometimes
weakens unduly the resemblance that exists between some of his
invented characters and their historical originals.

To work successfully the charade requires from us only that
we find *plausible* the identity which the actor contrives to
present, but this plausibility seems to me to falter at points. The
link between a wan and marginal figure like Deschamps and his
intense and anguished historical 'double' (Camille Desmoulins)
is too tenuous to be persuasive, and the same is true of the
relationship between Victoire and Lucile Desmoulins and that
between the vacuous Amanda and Madame Tallien, who was
one of the most resilient of the Revolution's survivors. More
convincing, in terms of dramatic impact are the affinities of
class and temperament which Anouilh evokes in the cases of
Brassac/Tallien and Vulturne/Mirabeau. On the other hand,
one feels a certain sense of strain and incoherence in the linkage
we are offered between Maxime's furious and self-interested
defence of the existing political order and Saint-Just's cold
revolutionary zeal, even when one recognizes the destructive
passion they have in common. A similar sense of uncertainty
attaches to our response to the doubling of Julien and Danton,
since though we acknowledge the relish for life they both
possess, Julien is quite without Danton's huge creative energies
and identifies himself with the existing social and economic
order in a way that makes nonsense of Danton's own
revolutionary activities. This comes out most obviously in
Julien's violent and rancorous dismissal of the poor: 'Il faut

absolument que je tue du pauvre ce soir... Mort aux faibles!
Qu'on le crie enfin! Mort aux misérables!' (p.124). As for Bitos
himself, Anouilh pushes our complicity as spectators very far
(because he is counting on our conservative response) when he
calls for us to identify a charismatic revolutionary like
Robespierre with this odious but minor agent of a Resistance-
dominated government. So I would argue that too great a gap
opens up between 'face' and 'mask' in *Pauvre Bitos*.

This lack of persuasive coincidence between certain of the
twentieth-century characters and the Revolutionary personages
they are called on to embody, emphasizes still further in *Pauvre
Bitos* the impossibility of viewing 'character' as other than
precarious, other than mere impersonation. In such a context,
character is not a life conceived in all its richness and complexity
but simply a vehicle for conveying arguments in a debate about
the perils of fanatically held convictions of a moral or political
kind. The schematic pattern of this debate is faithfully reflected
in the almost symmetrical disposition of the major characters,
and this is already apparent in Act I. Much of this act is taken up
with setting the scene for Maxime's dinner party. Conversation
among the early arrivals is used as a way of disclosing Maxime's
plot to humiliate Bitos, establishing Bitos's identity, and
providing us with the necessary background about his Resistance
loyalties and his work as a public prosecutor in the post-war
purge trials. But very soon after Bitos's entry (p.46), the debate
about political extremism is sharply engaged and draws some of
its force from the not yet fully realized traffic between the
present and the Revolutionary past. Bitos's solitary defence of
revolutionary politics is formally balanced by the arguments of
Maxime, Vulturne, Julien and Brassac. This pattern is repeated,
though with greater intensity and elaboration of the arguments,
in the dream of the second act. With the third act, the play veers
toward the farcical treatment of individuals so that the rather
schematic structure of argument which dominates Act II is
simply abandoned.

The characters, notably those of Act II, who emerge from this
symmetrical framework of debate are primarily 'voices' that
carry the burden of the arguments, but they also recognizably

belong to Anouilh's existing family of stage types, in some cases illustrating the device of self-quotation we have seen at work in *L'Alouette*. At the margins of the action, Charles and Joseph, the two prison warders of Act II of *Pauvre Bitos*, unmistakably echo the guards in *Antigone* with their gossip about rates of pay, postings and promotions. Just as Antigone's guard remains blithely oblivious to her anguish as she waits for death, and dilates enthusiastically on his special allowances — '... et, pendant six mois, à titre de gratification, un rappel de supplément de la solde de sergent...' (*NPN*, pp.197-98) — so Charles remains perfectly indifferent to the fate of the victims of the Terror as he sagely computes the comparative advantages of serving in the Force or Luxembourg prisons (pp.73-74). Warders and guards alike conform to Anouilh's caricatural image of the working classes. They lack tact and imagination and are the grossly insensitive, servile and mindless agents of state power. What the Prologue says of the guards in *Antigone* (*NPN*, p.133) — 'Ce sont les auxiliaires toujours innocents et toujours satis-faits d'eux-mêmes, de la justice' — finds its echo in Joseph's casual disavowal: 'Ça, c'est de la politique. Nous, on fait notre travail, c'est tout. Danton, non plus, il nous avait rien fait. Mais il y avait l'ordre: on l'a arrêté quand même. Nous, on fait ce qu'on nous dit...' (p.77). In the heavily stylized world of Anouilh's theatre, the working classes are, in their public lives, the passive tools of state tyranny and, in their private lives, drunken, promiscuous and violent. There is little sign of aware-ness that the criticisms applied to the guards might also apply to higher civil servants or the judges who preside over 'people's courts'. The picture we are given of Bitos's family life in child-hood simply reinforces this image: it is one of moral squalor in which his drudge of a mother has a succession of lovers and his father regularly beats him. This factitious and impoverished image of working-class life recurs in the aristocratic Vulturne's story of the gamekeeper who thrashes his stupid sons every evening 'à l'heure des devoirs' (p.41), and surfaces again in Julien's argument that, in rejecting 'le laisser-aller, le désordre, la crasse...' (p.51), Bitos is repudiating that which is most characteristic of life among the lower orders. Later Bitos admits as much, pliantly accepting the image which his 'betters' have of his class of origin: 'Mais je n'aime personne. Même pas le peuple. Il pue...' (p.121). Nor can it be said that this crudely conventional picture of working-class manners is mitigated in any significant way by the rather pallid defence of the common people put into the mouth of the schoolmaster Deschamps in Act III when he equates 'le peuple, le vrai peuple' with 'la race qui ne fait que donner...' (p.108). This idealized stereotype comes too late and is too perfunctory to offset the distaste generated by earlier images of working people.

Such a caricature of the working classes cannot seriously be intended as a picture of social reality. Rather it is proferred as one term in the imaginative dichotomy about which Anouilh's theatrical world is constructed. More specifically, this crudely reductive rendering of working-class life as inevitably coarse and brutalizing is the necessary antithesis of another stereotype he exploits, that of an idealized aristocratic way of life marked by social poise, tolerance and a sure sense of style. In the play, this way of life embraces the merely decorative (painted dolls like Lila de Preuil and Amanda Forrest) and the heedless arrogance of men of the world who combine wealth and charm, power and formal good manners (Maxime de Jaucourt, Julien du Bief, Vulturne de Verdreuil, Brassac). It is the sense of style, evidenced in their caustic wit as well as in their talent for carrying off party games with panache, which is repeatedly contrasted with Bitos's humourlessness and clumsiness. It would be too much to say that their style *redeems* their viciousness, but the satiric verve they deploy tends to give them all the best tunes, especially when they are set against Bitos's pompous earnestness and self-pity, or against Deschamps's solemn good will.

This emphasis on the opposition between the graceful and the ugly, the poetry and prose of human responses, is in danger of displacing the realities of social and economic conflict. In such a picture, politics tend to be seen as a choice between styles of life in the narrowly aesthetic sense, and such a choice is essentially a form of escapism. It supports the view, argued by Vandromme (7, p.126) in a slightly different context, that Anouilh prefers the unchanging and simple notion of 'estates' to the variety and

complication of social classes, if only because he is so affected
by the horrors wrought in the name of the latter. The scene
invented by Anouilh, in which Robespierre is received by
Mirabeau (pp.80-86), epitomizes this tendency to view politics in
terms of a simplistic dichotomy between well-bred stylishness
and the gracelessness of the common people. Robespierre who
was, in fact, a successful provincial lawyer at the time of this
imagined encounter, behaves like a raw boy, throws a tantrum
and spits on Mirabeau's drawing-room carpet. By contrast,
Mirabeau is shown to be the acme of courtesy, though a courtesy
tinged with infinite condescension. The stage directions are quite
explicit here: he is *'élégant et léger dans sa lourdeur...'*; *'il est à
l'aise...'*; *'il lui désigne gracieusement un siège...'*; *'[il] a un geste
gracieux...'*, etc. (p.81). And after Robespierre has spat on the
carpet, Mirabeau proposes to accompany him to his carriage in
order to demonstrate that revolution is not incompatible with
ceremonious civility (p.86). It is fair to say that Mirabeau's
blinkered and condescending paternalism does not escape
wholly unscathed from this episode, but the dramatic balance of
the scene is certainly tilted against Robespierre and leaves us
with a deeply unsympathetic image of him, even though he is
urging the just claims of the poor.

This way of seeing the conflict between social classes in terms
of a schematic opposition between grace and ugliness overlies
equally stylized divisions between rich and poor, moderates and
fanatics. So far as the division between rich and poor is
concerned, it tends to run counter to the feelings of sympathy
which Anouilh tries to elicit for his aristocrats by identifying
them as creatures of taste and sensibility, even if they are subject
to many lapses. The plain fact is that in *Pauvre Bitos*, as in a
number of Anouilh's earlier plays (*L'Hermine*, *L'Invitation au
château*, *La Répétition*), poverty degrades but wealth
dehumanizes. The poor may be very unattractive in their state of
humiliation, but the rich are callous in the exercise of their
power. However, such a sharp distinction between a class of rich
people endowed with taste and style, and a class of poor people
lacking both, also suggests the perpetuation of an unchanging
social hierarchy. Bitos's own pathetic account of being bullied at

school by his social superiors and of seeking to ingratiate himself with the aristocratic Maxime (p.62), implies that all social relations are frozen in a permanent antagonism between 'estates'. In such a context, the poor are doomed impotently to hate the rich and the rich fated endlessly to despise the vulgarity of the poor. As Maxime says to Bitos by way of explanation of his attitude toward him: 'Vous manquiez de grâce' (p.62). Oddly, this changeless pattern seems almost to be acknowledged by Bitos when he affirms: 'Si un jour j'ai droit à des armes comme vous, messieurs, il y aura les deux bras rouges de ma mère — croisés dessus' (p.63). This comment is balanced uneasily between being a vindication of the dignity of labour and an expression of social envy. Its effect is to consolidate the picture of a 'frozen' society which is implied in what Anouilh writes. Essentially it remains a glib rhetorical gesture included so as to condemn Bitos's ambition rather than to sympathize with his dilemma. Indeed, one is forced to ask how such an aspiration can be legitimate for a self-styled democrat, or even practicable since he serves a Republic in which hereditary honours no longer exist.

As for Anouilh's tendency to set moderates and fanatics in opposition one to another, one can see this at work in the way in which he balances Vulturne/Mirabeau, Brassac/Tallien and Julien/Danton against Bitos/Robespierre. In the figure of Vulturne/Mirabeau the virtues of aristocratic refinement are fused with those of political moderation, and the corrupt or compromised are defended as less dangerous to the world than the incorruptible who are convinced of their mission to save mankind (p.59). In addition, Vulturne defends the idea that 'true revolutions' are gradual (p.58), though, characteristically, he shows little awareness that revolutions are not automatic, and none of how they are to be started if all people share his view that nothing can be done anyhow. In the unaristocratic personage of Brassac/Tallien, the plutocrat and opportunist is offered as the new hero of our time since his desire for business as usual makes him the natural enemy of murderous idealists who wish to turn society upside down: 'Oui, les pourris, les vendus, c'est moi, ma chère; au milieu de ce troupeau de grands

idéalistes' (p.37). At one level, when Brassac gibes at Bitos for
being a social climber because he has not stayed in the class in
which he was born, the rich man's self-interest is so grossly and
openly expressed as to discredit him. But, at another level, his
criticism of the bloody consequences of political 'idealism'
strikes home, even if it is not delivered by a representative of the
true nobility. In implying that Bitos ought to remain faithful to
his class, Brassac seeks, at one and the same time, to embarrass
the former scholarship boy and to defend the *status quo*. It is an
impudent tactical move in the war against political radicals, but
it is one of the ironies of Anouilh's play that this breathtaking
cynicism is certainly more acceptable to us than the unctuous
advice offered by Victoire (Act III, p.130): 'Restez vous-même.
Restez pauvre!' Here the rich counsel the poor to be content
with their lot, but if money is so corrupting, why does the
priggish Victoire maintain such solidarity with her class?
Poverty freely assumed brings its own dignity, as Anouilh was to
show in *La Sauvage*, but when it is simply the function of an
unjust society, it remains an affront to human dignity. It is
doubtful whether Victoire or Anouilh recognize this. It is true
that the dramatist tries, in a very uncertain way, to raise her
above the other cardboard figures of femininity in the play, but
he does not seem to me to succeed. It might be said that Lucile
Desmoulins alone challenges the nullity of the women
characters, both in her complete devotion to Camille and in the
eloquence with which she defends the nurturing power of
women over the destructive appetites of men who never grow
out of being vicious schoolboys. Victoire remains an accomplice
in the process of humbling Bitos and though her warning to him
to avoid going to the night-club is an act of charity, it is not
enough to establish her as a figure of true compassion.

Danton is offered as the apotheosis of moderation to set
against Robespierre's fanatical pursuit of principle. In
upholding the virtues of private life, as distinct from the duties
and responsibilities of public life, Danton is, in some degree,
depoliticized by Anouilh and made into the life-affirmer who
contrasts almost symmetrically with Robespierre's life-denier.
Indeed, his eulogy of 'Les métiers, les enfants, les douceurs de

l'amitié et de l'amour' (p.95) is characterized by Saint-Just as counter-revolutionary. This is reminiscent of the treatment accorded to Danton in Georg Büchner's classic play *Dantons Tod*. The very grossness which is satirized by Anouilh in many of his portraits of the common man appears to be rendered sympathetically in the case of Danton. Julien, who is impersonating Danton, is allowed in Act I to express unalloyed relish for the pleasures of the table: 'Danton la grande gueule! Attends que j'avale. J'en ai plein la bouche de la ballotine de l'ami Tallien...' (p.51). Elsewhere, in Act II, the revolutionary Danton is the champion of the joys of women and drink. But the inconsistency here is more apparent than real. In this play, Danton's sensual nature is not viewed in the same light as the mean animality of the prison warders, the rough appetites of the soldiers in *Antigone*, or the crass self-indulgence of the petty-bourgeois parents of the early plays. If anything, it resembles the prodigality, the conspicuous consumption of the nobility of the Ancien régime, and this effect is strengthened for us because Danton is being played by a 'real' aristocrat (Julien du Bief). In affirming and celebrating life, Danton's appetites are presented as a wholesome antidote to the life-denying puritanism of Robespierre. They are the mark of a human, if deeply flawed, moderate; something that sets him apart from, and above, the anaemic rectitude of a principled but murderous zealot. In this sense, Julien/Danton's grossness, while embellishing (as in Büchner's play) the known facts about the historical Danton, raises his physical nature to the level of a metaphor about the preciousness of sensual appetite in a world of dehumanizing ideology. It is a device which helps to sustain that moral and dramatic dichotomy between moderation and fanaticism which is central to *Pauvre Bitos*.

The treatment of Bitos/Robespierre is, of course, crucial to the elaboration of this dichotomy, and tends to one satirical end: the discrediting of Bitos and his reduction to an odious figure of fun. There are, admittedly, isolated moments when the character of Robespierre is allowed to attain a certain kind of sinister grandeur, as when he defends the 'sacred' will of the people: 'Lorsque le comité de Salut public prend des décisions

qui peuvent te paraître arbitraires, il les prend pour le bien du
peuple...' (p.92), or when he condemns its frivolity: 'Il y a dans
ce peuple une incurable propension à la facilité et à l'insouc-
iance. Il accepte ses maîtres, mais il ne les respecte pas...'
(p.100). But Bitos himself is almost never permitted to reach
these equivocal heights. Perhaps only when he is replying to the
excuses of Franz Delanoue, petty criminal and 'poor little rich
boy', does Bitos strike a note of true moral indignation and pity
appropriate to the crisis of the times. It is when he counters
Franz's complaints of parental neglect with a fierce allusion to
the fate of the deportees during the German occupation of
France: 'Les fils des déportés des camps allemands n'ont-ils pas
eux aussi vécu comme des orphelins?' (p.69). Here, at least, one
feels that some sense of proportion about degrees of suffering
finds its way into the text. More characteristically, when Bitos
echoes the nostalgia for the lost innocence and exigent purity of
adolescence which is movingly, if sentimentally, expressed by
Lucile Desmoulins (pp.98-99), he contrives to taint it with
maudlin self-pity: 'J'aurais voulu que tout soit net, toujours,
sans ratures, sans bavures, sans taches...' (Act III, p.121). Quite
simply, Bitos/Robespierre is handled most of the time by
Anouilh in such a way as to excite our mistrust and loathing, so
that *Pauvre Bitos* emerges, as Vandromme has argued (7,
p.121), as a corrective to the dangerous moral absolutism that
can arise from an individual's experience of cruel humiliation. It
recognizes, and obliges us to recognize, the murderous
possibilities latent in the ethical rebellion of characters like
Thérèse in *La Sauvage*, whom we were originally invited to
admire, once their private revolt has been transposed into
public, and specifically political, acts.

The process of diminishing Bitos/Robespierre and the
ideological values associated with them takes a variety of forms
in the play. For example, Bitos's political ideology is shown to
derive from a simplistic belief in inevitable progress which
makes him clumsy and naive when set against the sophistry of
his tormentors. He tends also to be depoliticized, as well as
diminished, by the scenes of drunkenness and flattery which
occur in Act III, if only because his political principles emerge as

uncertain and fragile when contrasted with his gawping pleasure at finding himself in 'high society', and his snobbish and truly odious condescension toward the farcically named garage mechanic Fessard — 'le paysan du Danube', as he derisively christens him — who is touchingly concerned about Bitos's safety. The effect of this last stroke is to reveal just how uncertain is Bitos's commitment to the class from which he has sprung. It is an effect that is reinforced when he appears to hesitate and be tempted by Brassac's offer of a lucrative directorship. The sincerity of Bitos's political idealism is further impugned by Lila's gossip (p.38) about his having requisitioned the flat of a former collaborator in order to install his sister in it.

In surrounding the character the Bitos with so much denigratory detail, and in making him a figure of farce, Anouilh effectively deprives him of moral stature and depicts him as deeply unappealing, and this in spite of the fact that his antagonists are themselves so very unattractive. But the object of devising moments which will convince us in dramatic terms of the truth of this image of Bitos is not simply to discredit him as a person. The aim is to persuade us that it is impossible for the advocates of revolutionary change to be viewed except in terms of vulgar self-interest and serious psychological deficiencies. All dreams of bringing about radical change in society, and any sense that such dreams might derive from a desire to enlarge human happiness and reduce injustice and humiliation, have to be shown to emanate from emotional cripples or from resentful and ambitious climbers angry at being denied privileges they covet for themselves. In the case of Bitos, this strategy not only requires that his love of the common people should be exposed as less than disinterested and based on a convenient abstraction (the idealised *peuple*), but also that his political principles should be seen to be rooted in his twisted personality.

All this is vividly illustrated in the episode (p.39) devoted to the execution of the young *milicien*. This is not enacted, like the inner plays of *L'Alouette*, but simply reported at second hand by a hostile and ironic narrator (Julien). In his account, every-thing is recalled in such a way as to reduce the complicated moral dilemmas and ambiguities of resistance and collaboration

to vulgar melodrama in which the roles are schematically
distributed between victim and 'executioner' (in the sense that
Bitos emerges as morally responsible for Lucien's death).
Collaboration is rendered, if not harmless, at least as marginal;
a youthful misdemeanour rather than a political allegiance the
consequences of which might include the imprisonment, torture
or death of other Frenchmen. There is no interest in exploring
motives or causes. The potential richness that might come, in a
more naturalistic model of playwriting, from probing the
complexities of the moral and emotional responses of
individuals is deliberately sacrificed to a clash between cursorily
delineated stereotypes embodying respectively vulnerable and
immature youth and callous political zeal and ambition.

We discover that the victim learned his catechism in the same
class as Bitos, a detail rather too obtrusively planted so as to
excite a sentimental response to the innocence of childhood, yet
we are never told what Lucien actually did as a *milicien*. Given
the ugly record of the *milice* in war-time France, that is a
significant omission, or would be if Anouilh were concerned
with 'realistic' character portrayal. He is not. Consequently,
what we get is the interplay of theatrical stereotypes handled in
such a way as to invite our loathing and contempt for the
'villain' Bitos, who emerges as a dangerous and repulsive
political zealot. Julien's narration is shaped so as to pass from
intimations of childhood innocence (preparation for first
communion) to those of man's inhumanity to man (death by
firing squad). To round off the picture, the indirect agent of that
execution has to be shown, in a kind of black cartoon, as a
monster of maudlin sentiment, quite devoid of moral tact or
delicacy, when he buys an expensive doll for the dead man's
little daughter: 'Une poupée qui fermait les yeux et disait papa et
maman' (p.39). This detail is positively grotesque and owes
more to Anouilh's professional instinct for creating clinching
theatrical images (a fatherless child listening to a doll saying
'daddy') than to any sense of psychological plausibility. It
works, if at all, only at the level of caricature. I am left with the
feeling that the entire episode has slipped out of the dramatist's
aesthetic control and that he has failed to distance his hatred of

the French political Left. Far from being neutralized in emotional terms by Julien's ironic qualification of Bitos's action — 'Et d'ailleurs, Bitos n'est pas un assassin, c'est un magistrat; il ne faisait, en principe, que son devoir' (p.40) — the significance of the episode is savagely reinforced.

Julien's ironic report, placed where it is, early in Act I, necessarily determines our judgement of Bitos even before he arrives on stage. It is a legitimate dramatic effect and establishes Bitos as a contemptible figure who combines cant and inhuman political zeal. More than that, it obliges us to connect Bitos's revolutionary ideology with serious psychological weaknesses, those that are manifested by the ease with which he passes from a kind of arid legalism to gross sentimentality and self-pity. I suppose it could be said that though Bitos's purchase of the doll is quite excessive as a dramatic effect, it is, at least, consistent with the self-pity he exhibits for his own abused childhood. The wounds of childhood are, in fact, used to explain, or rather explain away, the politics of both Bitos and Robespierre. For Bitos, innocence or purity are not what are actually experienced in childhood but craved for in the midst of a family life marked by physical abuse, personal humiliation and moral squalor. Certainly Bitos's own childhood is not invested with the sort of radiance and pathos we meet in *Antigone*. On the contrary, it is, as Borgal has persuasively suggested (*11*, p.159), the matrix of dreams of violence and power demanding urgently to be satisfied in the adult world.

This is also true of Anouilh's portrayal of Robespierre in Act II where the treatment of his boyhood is one of the ways exploited by Anouilh to discredit and dismiss the revolutionary politics of the adult Robespierre. Here I am not always convinced that the trick of identifying Bitos with Robespierre wholly works. Too frequently, it seems to me, the disparity between the moral and intellectual stature of the two characters is too great, and the powers they respectively command too unequal to offer a credible comparison. After all, Bitos is never more than a minor agent of the central power while the historical (and stage) Robespierre is himself that power, just as he is the architect of policy and the arbiter of life and death. In this sense,

Anouilh raises, in the figure of Robespierre, expectations that are beyond the capacity of Bitos to fulfil. To some degree, Robespierre emerges as the folk-demon to match Joan of Arc's folk-heroine, but Bitos certainly does not occupy that commanding and malevolent position in French provincial society after the Liberation. Robespierre as folk-demon fits neatly into the conventionally simplified picture of national history that Anouilh draws upon, but for an explanation of the phenomenon that Robespierre was, the dramatist resorts to a glib and rather crude form of popular psychology. One can see this at work in several episodes.

When, in Act II (pp.78-81), Robespierre is beaten at college by his form-master in order that his wilful pride may be broken, Anouilh inserts two details which, somewhat too transparently, 'explain' Robespierre's subsequent political extremism by reference to this boyhood encounter with authority. In the first, the stage directions specify that the Jesuit schoolmaster should look like the king: '*Le régent du collège — un Père jésuite qui a les traits du roi...*' (p.78). In this way, Robespierre's subsequent involvement in regicide can be presented as the natural, and perhaps inevitable, need to revenge himself on those who humiliated him in youth. The second detail occurs when the beating is over and the Jesuit priest has left the room. Here again the stage direction are explicit: '*Quand il est sorti Robespierre va jusqu'aux verges; il les regarde, les touche du pied, puis les ramasse du bout des doigts avec une sorte de curiosité effrayée et les repose*' (p.80). This time the discarded canes resemble the *fasces*, those bundles of rods that were the emblem of power and authority in imperial Rome. Robespierre's fascination with them betrays a mixture of attraction and repulsion and looks forward to his own severe exercise of repression during the Terror. There is no denying that these constitute a deft and vivid piece of symbolism but the effect is to reduce political motivation to little more than compensatory fantasy. It works theatrically but is altogether too neat and superficial as an explanation of the reasons which drive men to adopt a particular political ideology.

In a comparable way, Danton is shown as humbling Robespierre in a bout of horseplay (pp.94-95), a scene which prefigures, and supplies the psychological basis for, Robespierre's later decision to have Danton executed. The implication is clear: Danton will go to the guillotine not for complex, and no doubt extreme and misguided, reasons of policy, but because Robespierre has to avenge himself on his tormentor, on the Danton whose bear-hug has made him look a weakling in public. The effect here again is to diminish Robespierre. By explaining Robespierre away in terms of his psychological need to take revenge on those who have previously humiliated him, Anouilh does in fact *depoliticize* him. Elsewhere the process of diminishing Robespierre takes the form of poking fun at his puritanism, as when Danton mocks him: 'Bois tout de même, petit curé' (p.89), or of repeatedly showing his nervous tic of brushing himself down, a sign of his neurotic compulsion to cleanse a soiled world. Similarly, Robespierre's crucial monologue in Act II (pp.99-100) is altogether too explicit an attempt to account for the architect of the Terror in terms of his emotional and sexual inadequacies. His fierce outburst against the 'beaux mâles' again tends to depoliticize him and to make all history the tale of the psychological maladjustments of those who rule. All aspiration beyond the commonplace has to be presented as sick or, at the very least, suspect. The roots of Robespierre's *political* activity have to be shown to lie in the stored hatreds and resentments of a timid man for those who have made him feel afraid or inadequate when he was powerless to check them: repulsive Marat and his charisma with the people; the contemptuous Mirabeau showing him the door; Danton with his brute strength and appetite for life; the teachers who beat him as a boy. Now, in the power given him by the Revolution, Robespierre is able to compensate for all this: 'Beaux Français, beaux messieurs, beaux mâles, je vous le ferai passer le goût de vivre et d'être des hommes! Je vous ferai propres, moi!' (p.100). There is, of course, a very self-conscious parallel here with what Bitos will say in Act III when he recognizes the fear he inspires in others: 'Le sentiment de vous faire peur, à tous, est doux aussi...Hein? Le petit Bitos qui était si comique tout à l'heure? On ne rit plus' (p.121).

In the melodrama of forces competing for power in Act II of

Pauvre Bitos, Anouilh allows Robespierre to claim the role of Virtue and to impute Vice to the moderate opposition, but he does so in order to create an ironic design the aim of which is to expose 'Virtue' as a monstrous perversion and 'Vice' as a saving grace. But the dramatic persuasiveness of this tends to be eroded as a result of Anouilh's preference for viewing Robespierre as a 'case'. The danger here is of making Robespierre, and Bitos too, pathetic victims of their complexes and not the frightening apostles of political ideologies who envisage the destruction of natural man so that the reign of virtue can be established in a new society. In presenting politics almost uniquely as the public enactment of private neuroses Anouilh leaves too much out of human experience. It is possible to describe societies quite objectively as oppressive and unjust. If men are led to change such societies and to support certain kinds of ideology in order to do so, the fact that their choices are strongly conditioned by psychological needs or failings does not affect the objective reality of oppression. Flawed and self-interested men are capable of serving causes greater than themselves and our interest in them may lie precisely in that contradiction. Anouilh's insufficient awareness of this encourages him to adopt an altogether too simple and schematic typology of characters in this play, even when such a typology is made dramatically effective.

No political ideology emerges unscathed from the fierce satire of *Pauvre Bitos*, though the excesses of the revolutionary Left are much more exposed than any others. There is little to offset the general misanthropy: those characters who are not hateful are too glancingly and pallidly represented to counter the bitterness, cynicism and despair generated in most of the play. This is a desolate theatre. As the final curtain falls on *Pauvre Bitos*, the cacophony of the car horns from the street outside underlines the overwhelming sense of moral and political discordancy reflected in the conflicts of the characters.

4. Conclusion

In the closed world of theatrical convention represented by
L'Alouette and *Pauvre Bitos* language is another form of
artifice, always subdued to the needs of dramatic effect and
contrast. There is almost nothing here of the naturalistic concern
with rendering the breaks, repetitions, hesitations and syntact-
ical lapses that are present in our everyday speech. In this
respect, what the Count wittily says in Act II of *La Répétition*
(*PB*, p.387) epitomizes Anouilh's dramatic practice:

> D'abord dans la vie le texte est toujours si mauvais! Nous
> vivons dans un monde qui a complètement perdu l'usage
> du point-virgule, nous parlons tous par phrases
> inachevées, avec trois petits point sous-entendus, parce que
> nous ne trouvons jamais le mot juste. Et puis le naturel de
> la conversation, que les comédiens prétendent retrouver:
> ces balbutiements, ces hoquets, ces hésitations, ces
> bavures, ce n'est vraiment pas la peine de réunir cinq ou six
> cents personnes dans une salle et de leur demander de
> l'argent, pour leur en donner le spectacle.

This plea for a stage language that is altogether more formally
ordered than the speech we encounter in life, and more fully
expressive, resourceful and stylishly alert, is precisely what the
plays respond to. Normally the idiom of *L'Alouette* and *Pauvre
Bitos* is not strikingly poetic or suggestive, but it is always alive,
full of satiric energy, and capable of a certain kind of ironic
allusiveness as well as of sustained passages of rhetorical power.
As a general effect, *L'Alouette* has much more variety of tone
and affective colour than *Pauvre Bitos* which often suffers from
a sort of hectoring monotony. Words in these plays tend to have
the energy of acts.

Only to a very limited degree are characters individuated

according to the language they use. Certainly, the language of the common people — Joan's father, La Hire, the prison warders of *Pauvre Bitos* — is intended in its coarseness and violence to mirror their unthinking brutality. To that extent, it reinforces Anouilh's conventional typology of character and lends to the plebs an almost primitive status.

Elsewhere, as Harvey perceptively notices (*17*, p.141), it is Anouilh's own tone of voice, own inventive and highly articulate language that tend to be generalized over his major characters. The distinctive features of this language are its hard edge, clarity and almost percussive force, combined with its gift for moving effortlessly from the witty and urbane, the elegant and pointed, to rhetorical expressiveness, studied invective, and open truculence. The dramatist may subdue himself so as to respect Joan's rustic simplicity and directness, though even here he coarsens her idiom in a way that is both anachronistic and inconsistent with the formulaic epithets he lavishes on her ('petite', 'pure', 'frêle', 'pauvre', 'grise') and which represent the language applied to the family of heroines to be found in many of his plays. On the other hand, it is Anouilh's own voice that soars over all others in *Pauvre Bitos* and lends to the major male characters a common style of utterance. They are all granted a capacity for lively insult and sarcastic irony and are all too uniformly endowed with wit and verbal resourcefulness to be quite plausible as individuals, as distinct from 'voices' in a debate. But such language is an integral part of the theatricalism that dominates the play.

Enough of the sense of innocence martyred by religious fanaticism and corrupt and implacable institutions survives in *L'Alouette* to enable one to say that the original legend, even if damaged at points by facility and vulgarity, retains much of its power to move us. In *Pauvre Bitos*, however, Anouilh's handling of the conflict between ends and means, extremism and compromise, tends to denature and degrade a potentially great and tragic subject by frequently reducing it to a sour farce rooted in personal spleen and vindictiveness. In *L'Alouette* it is Joan's detractors who cannot believe that her transcendent desire to serve God can reflect anything other than error, calculation or self-interest. In *Pauvre Bitos* the consistently low view of human motives and possibilities is crudely inflated and almost universally applied. Virtually everyone is infected with meanness of spirit. The tragic errors and confusions which spring from revolutionary idealism are displaced from the centre of our attention and drowned in a general misanthropy which leaves no principle or aspiration untouched.

Anouilh's vision of the world, bleak in *L'Alouette* and reduced to savage caricature in *Pauvre Bitos*, is embodied in a loud, busy and populous scene, conferring an unashamed primacy on the knowing manipulation of theatrical images, conventions and effects. As a theatre, Anouilh's is flagrantly self-referential: it winks at the audience and invites its complicity in the playing of a shared game. And this game, with its love of pretence and impersonation, its restless traffic between self and persona, actor and character, its interplay between illusion and reality, offers itself as the very image of human life. Within the context of the theatricalist technique he has inherited from the experimental theatre of the nineteen twenties and thirties (Pirandello, Salacrou, Roger Vitrac), Anouilh's own theatre emerges primarily as an art of embellishment superimposed on techniques that have become traditional, no matter how playfully he handles them. In these two plays, he stands out as a brilliant entertainer, combining enviable mastery of the resources of the stage with fierce and electric gifts as a comic moralist.

Select Bibliography

Kathleen White Kelly, *Jean Anouilh: an annotated bibliography* (Metuchen, New Jersey, Scarecrow Press, 1973).

A. EDITIONS OF ANOUILH'S WORK

Collected plays

Pièces noires (Paris, Calmann-Lévy, 1942). Post-war reprints: La Table Ronde.
Pièces roses (Paris, Calmann-Lévy, 1942). Post-war reprints: La Table Ronde.
  The 1963 edition includes for the first time *Humulus le muet*.
Nouvelles pièces noires (Paris, La Table Ronde, 1946).
Pièces brillantes (Paris, La Table Ronde, 1951).
Pièces grinçantes (Paris, La Table Ronde, 1958).
Pièces costumées (Paris, La Table Ronde, 1967).
Nouvelles pièces grinçantes (Paris, La Table Ronde, 1970).
Pièces baroques (Paris, La Table Ronde, 1974).
Pièces secrètes (Paris, La Table Ronde, 1977).

Uncollected plays

Y'avait un prisonnier (*La Petite Illustration*, 724, 1935).
Oreste (*La Table Ronde*, 3, 1945).
La Petite Molière (*Théâtre populaire*, 34, 1959).
Le Songe du critique (*L'Avant-Scène*, 243, 1961).
Mr Barnett (Paris, La Table Ronde, 1975).
Chers Zoiseaux (Paris, La Table Ronde, 1976).
La Culotte (Paris, La Table Ronde, 1978).
La Belle Vie, suivi de Episode de la vie d'un auteur (Paris, La Table Ronde, 1980).
Le Nombril (Paris, La Table Ronde, 1981).

Verse

Fables (Paris, La Table Ronde, 1962).

Articles and Interviews

A selection has been reprinted in:
Pol Vandromme, *Un Auteur et ses personnages* (Paris, La Table Ronde, 1965).

B. BACKGROUND TEXTS AND STUDIES

1. Robert Brasillach, *Le Procès de Jeanne d'Arc* (Paris, Gallimard, 1941: reprint 1950).

2. Georges et Andrée Duby (ed.), *Les Procès de Jeanne d'Arc* (Paris, Gallimard, 1973).
3. Norman Hampson, *The Life and Opinions of Maximilien Robespierre* (London, Duckworth, 1974).
4. *Ingvald Raknem, *Joan of Arc in History, Legend and Literature* (Oslo/Bergen/Tromsö, Universitetsforlaget, 1971).
5. Bernard Shaw, *Saint Joan* (Harmondsworth, Penguin Books, 1946).
6. M.J. Sydenham, *The French Revolution* (London, Methuen, 1969).
7. *Pol Vandromme, *Jean Anouilh: un auteur et ses personnages* (Paris, La Table Ronde, 1965).
8. Claude Vermorel, *Jeanne avec nous* (Paris, Editions Balzac, 1942).
9. Marina Warner, *Joan of Arc: the Image of Female Heroism* (London, Weidenfeld, 1981: reprinted Harmondsworth, Penguin Books, 1983).

C. CRITICAL STUDIES OF ANOUILH'S THEATRE

10. Bernard Beugnot (ed.), *Les Critiques de notre temps et Anouilh* (Paris, Garnier, 1977).
11. Clément Borgal, *Anouilh: la peine de vivre* (Paris, Editions du Centurion, 1966).
12. *Elie de Comminges, *Anouilh, littérature et politique* (Paris, Nizet, 1977).
13. *Alba Della Fazia, *Jean Anouilh* (New York, Twayne Publishers, 1969).
14. Hubert Gignoux, Jean Anouilh (Paris, Editions du Temps Présent, 1946).
15. *David I. Grossvogel, *20th Century French Drama* (New York/London, Columbia University Press, 1961), pp.147-204.
16. *Jacques Guicharnaud, *Modern French Theatre*, rev. ed. (New Haven, Yale University Press, 1967), pp.117-34.
17. *John Harvey, *Anouilh. A Study in Theatrics* (New Haven, Yale University Press, 1964).
18. *W.D. Howarth, 'Anouilh', in John Fletcher (ed.), *Forces in Modern French Drama* (London, University of London Press, 1972), pp.86-109.
19. ——, 'Anouilh and Molière', in W.D. Howarth and Merlin Thomas (ed.), *Molière: Stage and Study* (Oxford, Clarendon Press, 1973), pp.273-88.
20. S. Beynon John, 'Obsession and Technique in the Plays of Jean Anouilh', in Travis Bogard and William I. Oliver (ed.), *Modern Drama, Essays in Criticism* (New York, Oxford University Press, 1965), pp.20-42.
21. Dorothy Knowles, *French Drama of the Inter-War Years 1918-1939* (London, Harrap, 1967), pp.167-181.
22. Robert de Luppé, *Jean Anouilh*, rev. ed. (Paris, Editions Universitaires, 1961).
23. H.G. McIntyre, *The Theatre of Jean Anouilh* (London, Harrap, 1981).
24. Edward Owen Marsh, *Jean Anouilh, Poet of Pierrot and Pantaloon* (London, W.H. Allen, 1953).

25.   *Robert J. Nelson, *Play within a Play* (New Haven, Yale University Press, 1958).
26.   *Leonard C. Pronko, *The World of Jean Anouilh* (Berkeley, University of California Press, 1968).
27.   *Philip Thody, *Anouilh* (Edinburgh, Oliver and Boyd, 1968).
28.   Jacques Vier, *Le Théâtre de Jean Anouilh* (Paris, CDU/SEDES, 1976).

*Critical studies of particular interest.